A Sister's Shame

Also by Maggie Hartley

A Sister's Shame

TWO LITTLE GIRLS TRAPPED IN A CYCLE OF ABUSE AND NEGLECT

MAGGIE HARTLEY

SEVEN DIALS

First published in 2021 by Seven Dials,
an imprint of The Orion Publishing Group Ltd
Carmelite House, 50 Victoria Embankment,
London EC4Y 0DZ

An Hachette UK company

1 3 5 7 9 10 8 6 4 2

A CIP catalogue record for this book is
available from the British Library.

ISBN (Paperback): 978 1 8418 8478 3
ISBN (eBook): 978 1 418 8479 0

Typeset by Born Group
Printed and bound in Great Britain by Clays Ltd, Elcograf S.p.A.

www.orionbooks.co.uk

Dedication

This book is dedicated to Billie, Bo, Natalie and all the children and teenagers who have passed through my home. It's been a privilege to have cared for you and to be able to share your stories. And to the children who live with me now. Thank you for your determination, strength and joy and for sharing your lives with me.

Contents

A Message from Maggie

I wanted to write this book to give people an honest account about what it's like to be a foster carer. To talk about some of the challenges that I face on a day-to-day basis and some of the children that I've helped.

My main concern throughout all this is to protect the children that have been in my care. For this reason all names and identifying details have been changed, including my own, and no locations have been included. But I can assure you that all my stories are based on real-life cases told from my own experiences.

Being a foster carer is a privilege and I couldn't imagine doing anything else. My house is never quiet but I wouldn't have it any other way. I hope perhaps my stories inspire other people to consider fostering as new carers are always desperately needed.

Maggie Hartley

ONE

Mess and Stress

Putting his glass of shandy down, Graham reached for my hand across the table.

'I've missed you, Maggie,' he told me, giving it a squeeze. 'I really have.'

'And I've missed you too,' I smiled.

My boyfriend Graham was a calm, measured man and public shows of affection weren't usually his thing. They weren't mine either if I was being honest, so I was a little bit taken aback.

Graham was a physiotherapist and for the past six months he'd been working at a clinic that his friend Phil ran. It was a couple of hours away from where he lived, so he'd been staying with Phil and his wife four nights a week. Even though we'd been seeing each other for years, we still led quite separate lives. Graham was busy with his work and I was busy with my fostering and I didn't think it was fair to involve the children who came to live with me in my private life. Going out at night and at weekends was pretty much impossible for me so if we met up, it tended to be during the day if the children that I fostered were at nursery or school. We'd go for a walk or have lunch in a café. With Graham working away, we'd talked on the phone but we hadn't seen each other in person for weeks. Today he had a rare day off so we'd come for lunch at a country pub. It had been a while since we'd had time just to sit and chat and I filled him in on what was happening in my life.

'How's Louisa?' he asked.

'Thankfully everything seems to be going OK,' I told him. 'She's got a neat little bump and the baby is doing well.

'She's constantly on edge, though, which is understandable.'

'Poor girl,' sighed Graham. 'I really feel for her and Charlie.'

I'd started fostering Louisa when she was thirteen and her parents had tragically died in a car crash. She'd lived with me ever since, and I viewed her, to all intents and purposes, as my daughter. When she and Charlie had got married a few years ago, they'd moved into a flat ten minutes away from me and she still popped in all the time in between working as a nanny for a local family. Last year, she'd got pregnant and we had all been over the moon, but tragically, her twenty-week scan had shown that the baby, a little boy they'd named Dominic, had too many complications which meant that he wouldn't survive. Poor Louisa had been induced and had given birth to him before he'd passed away in her arms. She'd fallen pregnant again a few months later but even though tests had shown that what had happened to Dominic had simply been one of those terrible tragedies and wasn't genetic, she was still understandably anxious. She was sixteen weeks pregnant now, and I knew she was counting down the days.

2

'She still doesn't like to talk about the baby and she won't let me get any of the baby things they'd got for Dominic down from my loft,' I sighed.

When Dominic had died, Charlie had asked me to go and clear the nursery they'd decorated in their flat as he was worried it would be too painful for Louisa to see when she came home. All of the brand-new baby things were still up there gathering dust.

'And what about Natalie?' Graham asked. 'How's she doing?'

Natalie was the eleven-year-old that I'd been fostering for the past year. She'd been brought up by her grandmother, Peggy, as her mum, Donna, was an alcoholic who'd left when she was a baby. Unfortunately Peggy, who was sixty-five, had been diagnosed with Motor Neurone Disease. She'd deteriorated quickly and needed full-time carers, so Natalie had come into the care system. She still visited her nan several times a week, but I knew how upsetting it was for her to see her now, confined to a wheelchair and unable to speak.

'It's such a cruel disease,' I sighed. 'I know it's devastating for Nat.'

Life could be so cruel sometimes and my heart felt heavy for both of the girls and what each of them was going through.

We were so caught up in our conversation that I didn't hear my phone ringing in my bag. It wasn't until Graham had gone to the loo that I checked it and saw two missed calls. It was Becky's number – my supervising social worker from the fostering agency that I worked for.

'Something urgent?' asked Graham as he came back to the table.

'Oh, Becky's trying to get hold of me,' I shrugged. 'It's probably about the "skills to foster" course I'm helping them run next week, but I'd better give her a quick call to make sure.'

'Of course,' he nodded.

I quickly went outside to the car park and rang her. It was a chilly March day and I pulled my coat around me to protect me from the cold wind.

'Hi Maggie,' she said when she answered. 'Thanks for ringing back. I was hoping you might be able to help me with something . . .'

I could already tell by the serious tone of her voice that this wasn't about the fostering course.

'Social Services have just rung,' she told me. 'They're desperately trying to find a home for two little girls who've just come into care.

'I know you've only got Natalie at the moment, so I thought I'd try you.'

'What do you know about them?' I asked.

As was normally the case, the details were sketchy. The two little girls were four and seven and lived in a village around an hour away from me. Sadly, it sounded like a case of neglect.

'They haven't been in the area for very long, but a neighbour called the NSPCC because she was concerned,' Becky told me. 'The oldest girl doesn't seem to go to school and the neighbour has seen them wandering around the garden at all hours.

'She found the eldest walking on the road in the dark the other night. When she took her back, the parents didn't seem to even notice that she'd been missing and proceeded to hit her in front of the neighbour.'

When Social Services had gone to visit, they'd faced a hostile reaction. The parents wouldn't let them come in or see the children. The same thing had happened when they'd tried later the same day, so they'd applied to the courts for an Emergency Protection Order, or EPO, which meant Social Services could remove the children and take them into foster care if they had concerns. It also meant they could take a police officer with them who could force entry if the parents refused to let them in again. This time, however, they'd relented.

'When they eventually did get in, apparently they were living in absolute squalor,' Becky told me.

'Poor little mites,' I sighed. 'I'd be happy to take them.'

To be honest, I didn't even need to think about it. Cases where little ones had been neglected still broke my heart no matter how many times I'd seen it before.

'Thanks, Maggie,' Becky sighed, sounding relieved. 'I really appreciate that.'

'Oh, and you already know their social worker,' she added. 'It's a woman called Liz Fleming.'

'Oh yes, I remember Liz.' I smiled.

Liz and I had worked together a couple of times in the past. She was the social worker of a girl that I'd fostered years ago called Ruth whose story I told in *The Little Ghost Girl*, and, more recently, an eight-year-old boy called Tom who I wrote about in *Daddy's Little Soldier*. It was always nice when you had an established relationship with a social worker and I liked Liz a lot.

'I'll wait for her to bring them round then,' I told Becky.

'As far as I know, they spent last night in hospital being checked over, so she'll be bringing them to you from there,' she told me.

5

I went back into the pub to find Graham.

'You've got to go, haven't you?' he said as soon as I walked over to the table.

'I'm really sorry,' I sighed. 'A couple of children are on their way over to me and I need to make sure that everything's ready for them.'

'Don't worry,' he smiled.

I felt bad ending our lovely lunch so abruptly but Graham understood what fostering was like.

'Let's do this again soon,' he told me, as I bent down to give him a goodbye kiss.

'I'd like that,' I nodded, although with two young children on their way to me, I had no idea when that would be.

As I drove the twenty-minute journey home, I was filled with the rush of adrenaline I always got when a new placement was arriving. After years of fostering, I knew the routine by now, but I couldn't help but go through a mental checklist in my head. Natalie had one bedroom and the other spare room I used for foster children had a bunk bed and a single bed in it, so there was plenty of room for the girls.

Thankfully, there was already clean bedding on all of the beds. Recently I'd had older children staying with me so I'd made it look more grown-up, but with two younger girls on the way, I wanted to put some age-appropriate toys and books in there.

I'd built up a good stash of toys for all ages that I'd bought from car-boot sales over the years. I just needed to get them out of the loft.

Oh, and of course they'll need clothes, I reminded myself.

Little ones that had been neglected often tended to be on

the tiny side, so I needed to make sure I had some smaller stuff ready in case their usual sizes swamped them.

As soon as I walked through the front door and put my handbag down, I was like a whirlwind tearing round the house as I didn't know how long I'd have until Liz and the girls arrived. I swapped the duvet covers to some nice yellow spotty sets and put a couple of pink fleecy blankets and a little teddy on the end of each of the bunk beds. I always liked to do this with younger children as it often gave them comfort. I got a wooden dolls house out of the loft as well as some jigsaws and books and put them in their room. I got out fresh towels, purple toothbrushes and some princess toothpaste and rummaged through my cupboard to see what clothes I had for a four- and seven-year-old. Thankfully I had some underwear, pyjamas and a few basics that would tide them over until I managed to get to the supermarket to buy them some new bits and pieces.

After over an hour of dashing around, I was absolutely shattered. I was just about to put the kettle on and flop into a chair with a cup of tea when there was a knock at the front door. Clearly, the tea would have to wait.

I took a deep breath and went to open it.

'Hi Maggie,' grinned Liz. 'It's lovely to see you again.'

I remembered her distinctive red hair, which she'd had cut into a short bob since I'd last seen her.

'You too,' I smiled.

My eyes quickly moved to the two little girls standing on either side of her. My expectations of the children were so far from the reality in front of me that I had to stop myself from doing a double-take.

When a child has been neglected, they often come from a home where food is scarce and when they arrive on my doorstep they're usually painfully thin and skeletal. But neglect and malnourishment can take many forms, and these girls were the complete opposite.

The youngest one was almost as wide as she was tall. The leggings she was wearing were far too tight for her and her belly hung over the top of them. Her top was too short in the body and the material was stretched so tightly across her chest and upper arms, it looked like it was going to rip at any minute. I noticed she had a padded dressing on her chubby right hand. The older girl was just as rotund, her clothes straining at the seams, unable to cope with the tyres of flesh around her middle. Neither of them were particularly tall but they were both clearly obese. It was really sad and shocking to see young children this overweight.

They both had long, straggly dark hair, but neither of them looked particularly dirty. Their pudgy faces were sallow and they had dark shadows under their eyes, which were a really striking blue.

'This is Bo and she's four,' said Liz gently. 'And this is her big sister Billie, who's seven.

'Girls, this is Maggie who you're going to be staying with for a while.'

I bent down to their level.

'It's nice to meet you both,' I smiled. 'I've got lots of toys in my kitchen. Would you like to come in and see them?'

They both stared at me blankly, neither of them saying a word, their bloated faces completely expressionless. Liz ushered them into the hallway.

'Let's all go into the kitchen and I'll get everyone a drink,' I smiled. 'I don't know about you, Liz, but I'm desperate for a cup of tea.'

As they followed Liz inside, the two little girls seemed to waddle more than walk, and I could see that it was a struggle for them.

Poor kids, I thought to myself. *How could any parent let them get like that?*

'Girls, would you like some juice and a biscuit?' I asked them.

Although I could see they were overweight, I wanted them to feel as comfortable as possible, and biscuits normally went down well with young children.

Bo's eyes suddenly lit up.

'Wanna biccy! Wanna biccy,' she yelled in a voice that sounded much younger than her four years.

'Would you like one too?' I asked Billie and she nodded shyly.

I pointed out the toy cupboard to them before going to put the kettle on. I was just getting the juice out of the cupboard when I heard Liz suddenly cry out.

'Billie! No!'

I turned around just in time to see the older girl pull down her pants and leggings and squat down on the kitchen floor.

Please God, no, I thought to myself.

But before either of us could stop her, she proceeded to do a large poo on my kitchen floor. Without saying a word, she quickly pulled her pants back up and wandered off to look at the toys.

Meanwhile, Bo, who had been watching what was going on, came over to look at the deposit her older sister had left on the floor. Liz's mouth gaped open in horror as Bo put her hands straight into it and laughed as she swirled them around, creating a brown streaky mess on my tiles, almost as if she was painting a picture.

Liz looked as though she was about to pass out while I sprung into action.

'Don't worry,' I said in a singsong voice, grabbing Bo's hands and wiping off what I could with a handful of baby wipes that luckily happened to be out on the work surface.

'Let's take you to the toilet and get those hands clean,' I told her as I expertly guided her into the downstairs loo, making sure she didn't touch anything along the way.

I ushered her to the sink where I washed her hands several times with warm, soapy water and scrubbed her nails.

'You need clean hands if you're going to eat a biscuit,' I told her, keeping my voice light.

'Biccy,' she yelled. 'Wanna biccy now.'

'In a minute,' I told her. 'I just need to make sure your sister is clean too.'

Next, it was Billie's turn to be ushered to the toilet.

'In this house we use the toilet if we need to do a poo or a wee, lovey,' I told her.

I explained to her that she needed to wipe her bottom, otherwise she might get sore, and also that she needed to wash her hands.

She looked at me, clearly confused.

'There's the toilet paper,' I told her, pointing to it. 'Pull down your leggings and pants. I'll wait outside the door and you tell me when you're ready.'

She looked at me blankly like she hadn't got a clue what I was talking about, so I ripped off some toilet paper and, over my clothes, showed her how to wipe.

'Just like that,' I smiled. 'Then you put the paper down the loo. Flush it and then we'll wash your hands.'

She still looked hesitant, but as I waited outside the door I hoped she was doing as I asked. I was beginning to build up a picture of how these two little girls might have been living, as neither of them seemed to be familiar with using the toilet or hand washing.

I ushered Billie back into the kitchen. Bo was sitting on the sofa next to Liz, who was practically gagging at the smell in the room.

'Sorry, Maggie, I didn't know where any of your cleaning things were, so I haven't done anything about that.'

She gestured to the mess helplessly.

'It's OK,' I told her brightly. 'I'll sort it.'

I quickly put on my rubber gloves and got out some bleach and a bucket and cleaned the kitchen floor until it was sparkling.

'I'm so sorry, Maggie,' sighed Liz, coming over to me so the girls wouldn't hear. 'I forgot to mention the fact that both of them seem to go to the toilet wherever and whenever they want to.'

As if right on cue, Bo got up off the sofa and promptly weed through her leggings, all over the floor. My heart sank.

Yes, I thought to myself. *It was going to be a long day.*

TWO

Food wars

The girls had only been here twenty minutes and I'd spent most of that time cleaning. Liz and I hadn't even had time to have a proper conversation yet.

She offered to keep an eye on them while I dashed upstairs to get some dry clothes for Bo. I knew there was no way that she was going to fit into the age-four clothes that I'd got out for her, so I quickly went into my cupboard and found an age-nine dress that I hoped would be big enough. I also grabbed some age ten–twelve night-time pull-up pants that I'd found in the bathroom cupboard and prayed they would go over her legs.

'Just for now, to avoid any more accidents while we have a chat, I'm going to put her in these,' I told Liz, showing her the pull-ups.

'That's fine, Maggie,' she nodded. 'I don't blame you.'

I just hoped Billie didn't decide to relieve herself again.

Liz offered to change Bo in the downstairs loo while I got my bucket and bleach back out and tackled the puddle on the floor.

She looked exhausted by the time she staggered out of the toilet with Bo, who was now wearing the clean dress, which thankfully fitted her, though it was far too long.

'Right, let's get you both that juice and biscuit I promised you,' I smiled.

I put two beakers of juice on the table and handed them both a biscuit. Bo grabbed it and crammed it into her mouth. It was gone in seconds.

'More,' she shouted, crumbs spilling everywhere. 'Me want more.'

Billie had finished hers too, and had already rammed her hand in the tin and had shoved another couple into her mouth before I could stop her.

It had been a traumatic twenty-four hours for them and I wasn't going to tell her off. They didn't know Liz or me, they were in a strange new place and had been taken away from everything they knew. If an extra biscuit or two brought them comfort, then for now that was OK.

The sun had come out, so to give me chance to chat to Liz, I thought it might be nice for the girls to go out into the garden.

I opened up the patio doors.

'Would you like to have a play outside, girls?' I asked them. 'There's a sandpit out there, and swings and a slide too.'

Normally kids couldn't wait to get outside, but neither of them looked particularly interested. Slowly, they waddled after me and I showed them the sandpit and the buckets and spades I had in it. Liz and I could see them through the doors so we could keep an eye on them whilst still having a bit of privacy to chat.

Usually when new children arrived, they'd go out into the garden and run around or they'd kick a football or have a go on the swings. But the girls just stood there for a bit looking uncertain before they went and sat down in the sand pit.

'The poor things can hardly walk,' I sighed. 'How can anyone let a child get so big?'

'There was food in the house and I don't think they went hungry, but it was pretty much all junk,' Liz explained. 'I think they were just allowed to help themselves to whatever they wanted, whenever they wanted.

'I don't think either of them have been getting much in the way of nutrition or exercise.'

They'd been weighed and measured at the hospital and they were both several stone overweight for their age and classed as clinically obese. They also had a vitamin D deficiency, presumably from not getting outside enough, so they'd been given supplements to take.

'They're going to need lots of fresh fruit and vegetables, healthy meals and minimal treats as well as plenty of fresh air and exercise,' Liz told me. 'It's going to be hard and they're not going to like it, but hopefully over time their weight will slowly come down to a more healthy range for their age.'

I'd fostered overweight children before and sadly it was becoming increasingly common, but I'd never dealt with children who were this obese before. It was terribly sad as I could see their weight was impacting on their ability to do normal things that children do.

'So, what can you tell me about their parents?' I asked Liz.

Liz described how the children's mum, Mandy, was twenty-four and had learning difficulties.

'Like the girls, she's also very overweight,' said Liz. 'She was very quiet. While we were there, she hardly said a word.

'She just seemed very bewildered and overwhelmed.'

'And the dad?'

'There isn't a dad around,' she explained. 'Mandy's brother Jim lives with them.

'He was the one who did all the talking and was very aggressive and hostile. His exact words were, "I do my best to take care of Mandy because she's simple and she can't manage but I can't be watching her all of the f***ing time."'

I knew that learning difficulties didn't necessarily mean that someone couldn't be a competent parent. I'd come across many women with special needs who had become fantastic mothers. It was often just a case of giving them the right support.

Liz explained that Jim was a long-distance lorry driver and was away overnight a lot. He'd also told Social Services that Mandy 'was a bit of a slag' and had been 'knocked up by an old, married guy when she was a teenager' and that the girls both had different dads.

'He sounds charming,' I sighed. 'What was the house like when you got in there?'

'Oh, Maggie, it was horrendous,' said Liz, visibly shuddering at the memory. 'It was like something you see on one of those TV programmes about hoarders.

'There was stuff everywhere and it was filthy. Piles of mouldy dishes everywhere and rotting rubbish, dirty clothes, soiled bedding. There were three cats running round.

'The stench of urine and faeces was just unbearable. I'm not sure whether it was human or animal.

'It's an old cottage that apparently used to belong to their great-aunt, who recently died. It's completely run down, with old plumbing. The heating doesn't work and there are cracked window panes everywhere, so it was absolutely freezing.'

'Do you think either Mum or uncle are addicts?' I asked.

Liz shrugged.

'There was nothing to suggest that drugs or alcohol are involved. I think Mum's just never been taught how to be a good parent and is completely out of her depth in this dilapidated house.'

'It's a wonder the girls aren't more dirty,' I sighed.

'Oh, this is the cleaned-up version,' replied Liz. 'They were filthy. They had to give them a couple of showers each at the hospital just to get them into a clean enough state so they could be properly checked over.

'They were both caked in faeces and urine, so they were very sore and their clothes were horrendous. I nipped to ASDA on the way to the house but I didn't know then that they were so overweight, which is why nothing they're wearing fits.'

So far, all they knew about the family was that they had moved around the country a lot, never settling in one place for more than a few months. Social Services couldn't find any records for either girl at a GP practice, and as far as they knew, Billie had never been to school. Jim was paid cash-in-hand and the family weren't claiming any benefits, so perhaps that's why they'd managed to stay off the radar for so long.

'They moved into the house late last year after the great-aunt died, according to the neighbours,' said Liz. 'They saw the girls very occasionally in the garden. They said they were always barefoot, even in the winter, and dressed in flimsy clothes. They were outside at all hours.

'The neighbour was taking her dog for a walk the other evening when she found Billie wandering on the road in the dark. Again, she had no shoes and no coat.

'When she took her back, Jim apparently started shouting and swearing at Mandy for not noticing that she was missing and he was slapping Billie around the face. When the neighbour tried to say something, he swore and shut the door in her face.'

The neighbour had also noticed that Billie had a bad burn on her one of her hands that looked like it was infected.

'When they treated her at the hospital, she apparently told them she'd done it when she was playing with the gas fire,' sighed Liz. 'They've dressed it and she's got some antibiotics so we just need to keep an eye on it and check it's healing.'

'They were checked over medically, but developmentally, I suspect they're both very behind,' she continued. 'Bo has very limited speech and what she does say is what I'd describe as baby talk.

'Billie speech seems OK but she's seven and she's never been to school so she's got a lot of catching up to do.'

'So what happens now?' I asked.

'We'll continue our enquiries and while we do that, we'll go back to court and apply for an interim care order,' said Liz. 'I'll also try and arrange a contact session so the girls can see their mum.'

'What about the uncle?' I asked.

'Perhaps he might come to contact eventually but I think it will be good to see how Mandy is in sessions on her own with the girls first,' she said.

After we'd sorted out some paperwork, Liz had to go. She said goodbye to the girls and said she'd give me a call in the morning.

'You know where I am if you need me,' she told me. 'I hope they have a settled night.'

I did too.

After Liz had gone, I decided to show the girls their bedroom. Neither of them had come with any belongings at all.

'Let's go and see where you'll be sleeping,' I told them.

I started to head upstairs but when I reached the top and looked around, I realised the girls were really struggling. They were huffing and puffing and by the time they reached the top, they looked exhausted. It was heartbreaking to see them trapped in these overweight bodies. Children their age should have been running and jumping around, but even walking up the stairs left them breathless and panting. They were like prisoners in their own bodies and it wasn't fair.

They seemed to like their new bedroom well enough, although I was met with blank faces and neither of them said anything. When we came back downstairs, I decided to put the TV on for them. It would only be for half and hour and it would give me time to get dinner organised.

We went into the living room and I walked over to the TV and turned it on.

'Telly! Telly!' yelled Bo, her blue eyes lighting up.

As the screen flickered into action, I could see the look of relief on their faces as their bodies sank back into the sofa. I could tell by the glazed look in their eyes that this was something completely familiar to them. They didn't even seem to be particularly bothered about what it was they were watching. A daytime gardening makeover programme was on but they both seem transfixed.

'Would you like me to find you some cartoons?' I asked but neither of them responded.

I'd just gone out into the hallway, when I heard a key in the lock.

It was Natalie.

I quickly closed the living-room door.

'Hi, lovey,' I smiled. 'How was school?'

'OK, I suppose,' she sighed.

I quickly told her about the new arrivals and explained that they would be staying with us for a while. Natalie had been with me for long enough now that she was used to new children turning up without much warning.

'Cool,' she nodded. 'Can I say hello to them?'

'Before you do, there's something that I need to tell you,' I said.

I wanted to prepare her for the fact that they were obese. I knew it had been quite a shock for me and I didn't want her to say something in front of them.

'They're both quite overweight,' I explained. 'But they've not had access to proper food at their house.'

'Oh, that's sad,' said Natalie. 'Don't worry, Maggie, I won't say anything.'

I took her into the living room, where the girls were both still mesmerised by the telly.

'This is Natalie,' I told them. 'She lives here with me too and she's eleven.'

'Hi,' said Natalie, waving at them.

They stared at the TV, neither of them responding. I shrugged and led her out.

'Don't worry, flower,' I told her. 'They're both exhausted and they've had a really hard day.'

'You were right though,' she said, her eyes wide. 'They're really, really fat. How did they get like that, Maggie?'

'Probably a combination of things,' I shrugged. 'Not getting enough exercise and being inactive, eating unhealthy food.

'There might even be something medical that we don't know about yet. Whatever caused it, it's very sad for them.'

One thing that was going to be really important for the girls going forward was making sure they had regular mealtimes, and trying to get them out of the habit of endless eating, but I was dreading dinner time. In my experience, children who hadn't had proper mealtimes had not eaten at a table before and it was often a nightmare trying to keep them sitting down. I'd fostered sibling groups before where I was constantly up and down at meal times, retrieving children and bringing them back to the table. But because Bo and Billie were so overweight, they moved very slowly and they were very sedentary. They physically wouldn't be able to get themselves up and down quickly enough to leave the table.

When dinner was ready, I encouraged them both to sit down at the table like Natalie was doing, although they both looked very confused and unsure. First, I got everyone a drink. Water for me and Natalie, and milk for the girls because I thought they'd prefer it.

Bo pushed her beaker away.

'Don't want dat, want 'izzy! I want 'izzy! I want 'izzy,' she chanted.

I looked at Billie for guidance as I had no idea what 'izzy' was.

'She don't like that white stuff, she likes Fanta or 7Up or cola,' she told me matter of factly,

So 'izzy' must mean fizzy drinks.

'And she don't have it in that,' she said, pointing to the cup. 'She has it in a bottle.'

'Bokkle, bokkle, bokkle' shouted Bo.

'You don't need a bottle, Bo,' I smiled. 'They're for babies and you're a big girl. Four-year-olds drink their milk from cups.'

She shook her head.

'Me want 'izzy,' she said firmly.

'If you don't like milk then I'll get you some water instead,' I suggested.

'She don't like that neither,' said Billie. 'She only likes fizzy stuff.'

'I'm afraid we don't have fizzy drinks at mealtimes in this house,' I replied.

In a bid to distract them both, I started dishing up dinner. I'd wanted to give them something fairly plain and comforting, so I'd made shepherd's pie and peas. The girls eyed it suspiciously as I put the Pyrex dish down on the table.

'What dat?' asked Bo in her baby voice.

'It's called shepherd's pie,' I told her and as I served it up, I talked them through what it was.

'It's meat and peas and carrots and mashed potato and a little bit of cheese on the top.

'It's delicious, isn't it, Nat?' I said, nudging her for support.

'Yep, it's really tasty,' she smiled.

Both girls looks unconvinced as they stared at their plates with a disgusted look on their faces.

'Don't like dat,' sighed Bo. 'Me want crisps.'

'We don't eat crisps for tea,' I smiled. 'Not when we've got lovely shepherd's pie.'

'Choc choc?' asked Bo hopefully.

'Her favourite is Mars Bars,' Billie told me 'She likes them and she likes Milky Way and Snickers.'

'Don't want dis,' sighed Bo, pushing the plate away. 'Me want choc choc.'

She started to cry.

Billie rolled her eyes.

'For f***s sake, don't start, Bo Bo. F***ing shut your mouth.'

She said it in such a gruff, growly voice, it completely took me by surprise. She suddenly sounded far older than her seven years.

Natalie's eyes nearly popped out of her head.

'Billie, we don't do swearing in this house,' I told her. 'We don't use those words.'

'What's swearing?' she asked.

I could see by the innocent look on her face that she honestly didn't know. She hadn't been to school and I assumed she'd rarely mixed with other children.

'She means we don't say "f***ing",' Natalie piped up.

'Nat!' I scolded.

'Well, she asked what was swearing and I was only telling her,' she shrugged.

What Billie had said sounded like she was mimicking someone.

'What happens if Bo cries at home?' I asked her.

'If you want her to shush, you have to give her some chocolate or sweets,' she told me. 'She likes Haribos.'

'Is that what Mummy and Uncle Jim do?' I questioned and she nodded.

Bo refused to touch the shepherd's pie but Billie seemed to enjoy the few mouthfuls that she'd had.

After dinner, I could see they were both exhausted so I took them upstairs to get ready for bed. I already knew the pyjamas I'd got out for them wouldn't fit, so I got two bigger pairs out of my cupboard. Although they were large enough to fit over their legs and tummies, they were far too long in the legs and arms. I rolled them up but they still looked ridiculous. It would have to do for now. I also put them both in a pull-up, and thankfully neither of them objected. They were both so tired and I wanted them to have a comfortable, undisturbed night, so toilet training could wait until the following day. I just hoped that they would settle OK and manage to get some sleep.

When I checked on them fifteen minutes later, I opened the door to find that Billie had crept into Bo's bed and the pair of them were curled up together in the bottom bunk, fast asleep. My heart felt heavy with sadness for these two little girls who were prisoners in their own bodies. I was already building up a picture of how things had been at home for them – endless television and crisps and sweets to shut them up. And I knew there were probably more discoveries to come.

THREE

Rude Awakenings

The sound of my alarm clock woke me with a start. I sat up in bed and blearily looked at the clock.

7 a.m.

With a panic, I realised I'd slept solidly for eight hours.

Normally when new children arrive, I'm always very restless on their first night with me. I worry about whether or not they're going to settle and how they must be feeling to be in a strange place. Last night had been no different. As I'd got into bed, my mind had been whirring, thinking about Bo and Billie, but I must have been so exhausted that somehow I'd nodded off and fallen into a deep sleep.

It wasn't like me and I felt really guilty. But I was sure that if Bo or Billie had needed me and shouted out, I would have woken up.

Even so, I was keen to check that they were OK. I quickly pulled on my dressing gown and wandered down the landing to their bedroom.

My heart sank when I saw the two empty beds through the

open door. It sank even further when I saw the two discarded pull-ups and pyjama bottoms on the floor.

They weren't in the bathroom so I hurried downstairs, panic growing, unsure of what I was going to find. Much to my horror, what greeted me at the bottom of the stairs was a large poo. I glanced into the living room but the telly wasn't on and there was no one in there. I felt sick as I walked towards the kitchen, narrowly missing a puddle of wee.

At this rate, I'm going to run out of bleach, I thought to myself.

I pushed open the door to find Bo and Billie, both naked from the waist down and legs akimbo, sitting silently on the kitchen floor. The cupboards were open and Billie was clutching the biscuit tin in her lap and shoving custard creams into her mouth. Bo had found the large Tupperware box where I kept the crisps.

'Doritos,' she grinned at me, her mouth full.

I could see by the amount of empty wrappers that they'd been there for a while.

I wasn't going to tell them off as this was obviously what they were used to doing at home.

'Girls, you mustn't come downstairs in the morning unless I'm with you,' I told them gently. 'So when you wake up, you need to shout for me and I'll come and get you.

'Now, let's get you cleaned up before we have breakfast.'

I knew my first priority was to put a clean pull-up and some pyjama bottoms on them both. I got what I needed from upstairs and took them to the downstairs loo.

'Let's get you cleaned up,' I told them. 'We'll just pop you in a pull-up, wash your hands and then it will be breakfast time.'

I doubted they were going to be very hungry after all the food they'd already eaten, but it was more about trying to establish a sense of routine and getting them used to sitting at the table to eat.

We'd just walked back into the kitchen when Natalie came in, her face ashen.

'Maggie, did you know there's a poo on the floor in the hall?' she shuddered. 'It stinks.'

'Don't worry, I was just about to clean that up,' I told her. 'Along with the other puddle. If you could keep an eye on the girls while I do that, it would be much appreciated,' I told her in a low voice.

'That's fine,' she said.

I armed myself with my trusty rubber gloves, a bucket full of hot water and bleach, some kitchen roll and a mop. Before long, everything was gleaming again.

'OK then,' I smiled. 'Let's all sit at the table and have some breakfast.'

'Again?' sighed Billie. 'We did that before.'

'We always sit down at the table for our meals,' I told her.

'My mummy doesn't do it like this,' she said.

She and Bo did as they were asked but they sat there with a puzzled look on their faces as Natalie helped me put the spoons and bowls, a jug of milk and some juice on the table.

'What was your favourite breakfast at home?' I asked them both as I sat down.

They both stared at me like I was speaking a foreign language. I could tell that they had no concept about breakfast or any other mealtimes and what that meant.

'The food we eat in the morning after we get up is called

26

breakfast,' I explained. 'So we all come downstairs together and we can have cereal or toast or fruit or eggs.'

'Doritos?' asked Bo hopefully.

'No, in this house we don't have crisps for breakfast,' I told her.

I put a box of Frosties out on the table as well as some Weetabix and cornflakes. The Frosties were usually saved for a weekend treat but I knew the girls were more likely to eat something if it was sweet. I wanted them to get into the routine of meals as much as anything and to know the association of breakfast.

'Oh, I know that one,' smiled Billie as she saw the Frosties box. 'Mummy had that one time.'

I poured them each a small bowl but they sat silently staring, watching suspiciously as Natalie had her Weetabix and I had some toast, clearly unsure about this new thing called breakfast. In the end, they managed a couple of mouthfuls each, which was a success as far as I was concerned.

As Natalie helped me to clear the dishes away, I had a quiet word with her.

'I'm going to put all the crisps, biscuits and chocolates up into a high cupboard, and take any fizzy drinks out of the fridge,' I explained.

'Oh,' she said, her face dropping. 'Am I not allowed them any more?'

'You can still have them, lovey,' I told her. 'It's more so that Billie and Bo can't help themselves.'

Because of their weight, I knew I was going to have to be strict with food. I wanted the girls to get used to three meals a day, and if they wanted snacks, it was going to have to be crackers, fruit or rice cakes. It wouldn't be fair to stop Natalie having the odd treat, though, and as she was eleven and very mature for her age, I could trust her to be sensible.

After breakfast, it was time to give the girls a bath. They'd been too exhausted the previous night when they'd arrived. Even though they'd been showered at the hospital, their hair was greasy and lank and I knew a good soak in the bath would get rid of any lingering dirt.

I started running the water and put a big squirt of bubble bath in it before I helped them get undressed. As I saw them both stood there completely naked for the first time, tears pricked my eyes. It was upsetting to see how much extra weight they were both carrying and how uncomfortable and debilitating it must be for them. It was shocking to see the rolls of fat around their middles and the creases and dimples in their arms and legs like babies have. I suddenly realised that they probably wouldn't be able to lift their legs up high enough to climb into the bath and there was no way that I could lift them. Instead, I got the little stepping stool from my bedroom that I used to reach the high cupboards in my wardrobes.

Taking it in turns, I held their hands to help steady them as they climbed up the stool. Even those couple of steps were a struggle for them. Then slowly they sat down on the top and I helped to lower them into the bath.

I could see they were both relishing being in the warm, bubbly water.

I washed their hair a couple of times and then I got a flannel and gently washed them both, taking care to clean under all their creases and folds of skin. They were very sore under there and also on their legs where their thighs had chafed, and I wanted to make sure they didn't get any infections.

'We had a bath at home,' said Billie. 'But it wasn't fluffy and it made me go . . .'

She did a shivering motion.

'Oh, you mean the water was cold?' I asked and she nodded.

'I like this fluffy one much better,' she said.

I loved her description of the bubbles in the bath as 'fluffy' and I could see she was enjoying having a soak.

At the mention of home, Bo's ears suddenly pricked up.

'Go back now?' she asked me, looking worried.

'Where do you want to go back to, Bo?' I asked her.

'She means go back to Mummy's,' said Billie. 'When is she coming to get us?'

I didn't want to lie to them, but equally it was early days and at this moment in time I honestly didn't know what was going to happen.

'Remember the lady called Liz who brought you here yesterday?' I asked. 'Well, you're going to stay here with me for a bit while Liz chats to Mummy and makes sure everything is OK at home and if Mummy needs any extra help.'

The explanation seemed to satisfy them. It was hard for young children who had no concept of time and I knew from experience that it would hit them every now and again that their mum wasn't there.

While they were in the bath, it was also a good time for me to do a body plan map for my agency. This was a piece of paper with an outline of a body on it and I would make a note where any scars, cuts, bruises or marks of any kind were. It was important to record everything and I did one for every child that came into my care. These days, technology has developed so much that it's much easier to take a photograph on a mobile phone and email it to social workers (as long as it's in an appropriate place).

Billie still had a dressing on the burn on her hand so I'd put a rubber glove on it so it didn't get it wet.

'How's your hand doing, sweetie?' I asked her. 'What happened?'

'I put it on the fire and it was hot and made me go ouch,' she told me.

'Oh dear,' I sighed. 'Where was Mummy?'

Billie shrugged.

'I wanted the fire on cos it was cold.'

'You have to be very careful with fires,' I told her gently. 'Only adults should touch them, they're not for children to play with.'

While they were playing with the bath toys, I folded up their clothes. I was just getting their towels from the rail, when I heard Bo cry out behind me.

'No, Billie,' she whimpered.

Just visible under the bubbles was Billie's hand and she was pushing a dolphin bath toy between her sister's legs.

'Billie, what on earth are you doing with that bath toy?' I asked her, shocked.

'I'm poking it in Bo's noo noo,' she told me. 'She ain't bothered. She likes it, don't you, Bo Bo?'

'No!' shouted Bo, pushing the dolphin away.

I was completely taken aback.

'Billie, we don't do that,' I told her. 'We don't put things in people's noo noos. That's Bo's body and it's private. Come on, let's get you out,' I told her.

It was such a strange thing for a young child to do, and I reminded myself to make a note in my daily recordings that I sent to Liz.

After their bath, I got them dressed and back into a pull-up each. I knew I needed to toilet train them, but we had to go out to the shops this morning and I couldn't risk them relieving themselves on the floor everywhere we went. I didn't think I would be able to cope with toilet training both of them at the same time, so as soon as we had a few days at home, I was going to concentrate on Billie first. As she was seven and hopefully starting school soon, she was the priority. But for now, I was going to have to put them in pull-ups, and to my relief neither of them seemed to mind.

Our first job was a quick trip to ASDA to get them some clothes. Or at least, I'd planned for it to be quick, but sadly walking was a real effort for the girls and they moved extremely slowly. As I rummaged through the rails, I knew I had to think cleverly. There was no way they would fit in the sizes for their age, but on the larger sizes the legs and the arms were way too long. So I went for tops where I could roll the sleeves up and skirts with elasticated waists rather than trousers so I could fold the waistbands over if they were too long.

Next it was the shoe shop. It was a real struggle for the girls to bend down and get their shoes on and off, so I had to help them. As they put their feet down to be measured, I could see they were all swollen and their ankles were puffy.

The shop assistant couldn't conceal the look of disgust on her face as she measured their swollen feet. I knew her vitriol was aimed at me and she was wondering how on earth I had let these children get so big. It was times like these, or else when children were acting up in public, that I wished I had a special badge stating that I was a foster carer, to avoid the unkindness and judgment of strangers. They had no idea of the things these children had suffered. They were the victims in all this, and none of what had happened to them was their fault.

Although their feet were swollen, the girls could at least have a bit more freedom when it came to shoes, and they were both extremely excited at being allowed to choose for themselves. Bo wanted a pair of pink shoes which sparkled, and Billie opted for some that had flashing heels. It was clear they'd never been shopping for something before, and both of them were visibly fizzing with excitement as we finally left, laden with shopping bags.

The girls had been so well behaved and done everything I'd asked without complaining, so on the way home I decided to take them to the park. I thought they'd enjoy going on the swings, and the fresh air would do them good. It was a five-minute walk from the car park to the playground and the girls were gradually getting slower and slower. There was a slight hill on the way to the park and I could see Billie was completely out of breath as she waddled up it. Halfway there, Bo stopped dead in her tracks.

'Me want a buggy,' she panted.

'I'm tired,' wailed Billie.

I could see they were both utterly exhausted and I felt bad as this had meant to be a treat, not a punishment.

'You're doing really good walking,' I encouraged Bo. 'You're a big girl, you don't need a buggy.'

It took endless persuasion and lots of stopping and starting before we made it to the playground. The five-minute walk from the playground had taken us almost half an hour. Bo cheered up when she saw other children in the swings.

'Would you like a go, flower?' I asked her and she nodded eagerly.

But as we walked towards them, I realised the swings were ones with an enclosed seat and I knew I wouldn't be able to manage to lift her into one. Even if I did, there was no way that she would fit into it.

'Do you want to go on the big girl's swings instead?' I asked her, pointing to the other swings.

But she shook her head.

'I want dat one,' she said.

I tried to distract her with something else but the sad fact was that nothing in the playground was geared up for children of their size, and I kicked myself for not considering the impact their weight might have. They couldn't manage the steep steps up to the slide and would struggle to get down it at all. Neither of them were agile enough to go on the monkey bars or crawl through tunnels. The only thing they could manage to get onto was the roundabout, so that's what we did. They had twenty minutes of clinging on for dear life, giggling and squealing while I spun them round and round. They were both dizzy as anything by the time they'd got off, but at least they'd had a bit of fun.

By the time they waddled back to the car, they were both wheezing and exhausted. As I walked through the front door, my mobile was ringing in my bag. It was Liz.

'How are you, Maggie?' she asked. 'How are the girls doing?

'They're not too bad,' I told her. 'We've just got in actually.'

'I'm glad I've caught you,' she said. 'The hospital has just called. They got the results of the girls' blood tests.'

She paused.

'They've got rickets, Maggie.'

'Rickets?' I asked, puzzled. 'Isn't that something from the olden days? I didn't think people got that any more.'

Liz explained that in recent years, sadly, there had been a resurgence due to some children's diets being so poor.

'It's caused by a vitamin D and calcium deficiency,' she told me. 'It might also explain why they walk with a bit of a waddle, as their bones could be sore and painful. All that extra weight they're carrying certainly won't help.'

Unfortunately, there was no magical cure. The only things that could cure it were supplements, lots of healthy food, sunlight, fresh air and exercise.

Poor little loves. In my entire fostering career, I'd never known a child to have rickets before. I knew it wasn't for me to judge any parent, though. I didn't know yet what had gone on behind closed doors, and the reality was, it was easier and cheaper to feed kids junk food than it was to cook them healthy, fresh food. Perhaps Mandy didn't know how to cook, or she didn't have enough money to feed her kids? As I always said, I couldn't change a child's past or what had happened to them. All I could change was the future.

FOUR

Meeting Mummy

As I drove down the street, I was worried that I was totally lost until I saw the newly built bungalow in front of me.

'Here we are,' I smiled, pulling into the driveway.

It looked to all intents and purposes like any ordinary house. It was only the sign in the front garden saying 'Oak Lodge' and underneath in small letters the wording that said it belonged to Social Services that gave away its real purpose.

'Is this the place, Maggie?' yelled Billie from the back of the car.

'Yes, lovey, this is it,' I told her.

'Has it got toys?' she asked.

'I think it will have, although I've never been here before either, girls,' I told them as I parked up and we got out of the car.

Oak Lodge was a new purpose-built contact centre that had just opened, and it was where Billie and Bo were having their first contact session with their mum, Mandy. Liz had texted me earlier to say that Mandy was on her way and as it was a 45-minute drive from my house, I'd set off with the girls. We'd decided that it was best for us to arrive first and to get the girls settled before Mandy turned up.

'Is Mummy here?' asked Billie excitedly as I pushed open the front door.

'Not yet, lovey,' I told her. 'But hopefully she will be soon.'

As we walked into the entrance hall, there was a hatch to the left and a small office behind it. I pressed the buzzer and a young woman came to the glass screen. I showed her my ID and signed in.

'Liz is through there,' she told me.

She pressed a buzzer and a double set of security doors opened up. Contact centres were always very secure, to protect children's safety and to make sure people couldn't just wander in and out of them.

Liz was waiting for us in the hallway.

'Hello, girls,' she smiled.

'Well, this is all very nice,' I told her looking around. It still smelled of fresh paint and everything was gleaming and brand new.

'I know,' she nodded. 'It beats the pokey rooms in the Social Services building in town, doesn't it? It only opened last week. I can give you a quick tour if you want? I don't think Mandy will be here for another fifteen minutes or so.'

'That would be great,' I smiled.

Off the long hallway there was a large, bright kitchen with a dining table, several highchairs, a dishwasher, oven and washing machine. There were two toilets and a large bathroom with a bath.

'We can use the centre for mum and baby assessments so parents can come and spend the day here and look after their babies.'

'Oh, Maggie's got one of them,' said Billie excitedly as she saw the bath. 'Is it a fluffy one?'

Liz looked confused.

'The girls have been enjoying having bubble baths, which Billie calls "fluffy",' I explained, grinning.

'Oh, I see,' smiled Liz.

At the back of the house was a conservatory with doors opening out on to a large garden where there was a swing, a slide and a sandpit.

'It's really lovely,' I gasped. 'They've thought of everything.'

There were also three large contact rooms where parents could spend time with their children, although we seemed to be the only ones here this morning.

'Come and have a look at this room, girls,' said Liz, ushering them into one of them.

Like the rest of the house, everything was immaculate and it was really homely. There were baskets full of brand-new toys and books and a lovely squishy sofa and a couple of armchairs. The walls had been freshly wallpapered and there were lamps and a coffee table. Most of the contact centres I'd been to had been used for years and were run down. The furniture was grubby and the toys were well worn and falling apart, so this made a nice change.

'Did Maggie tell you why you've come here today?' Liz asked the girls.

'To see my mummy!' shouted Billie.

'Mummy!' repeated Bo.

'That's right,' replied Liz. 'So how about you have a look through the cupboard and choose some games that you think Mummy would like to play with you.'

Just then, an older woman who I would guess was in her early sixties walked into the room.

'Maggie, this is Janet,' Liz told me. 'She's going to be the contact worker supervising the sessions with Mandy.

'We won't need her today as you and I are here, but I thought it would be good for her to come and say hello to you and the girls.'

'Lovely to meet you,' Janet smiled.

While she introduced herself to the girls, Liz and I nipped out into the hallway. I had one eye on the clock and I was growing increasingly aware of the fact that Mandy hadn't arrived yet. Sadly, I'd been to many contact sessions where the parents didn't show up, and I knew how distressing that could be for children when they were expecting to see their mum and dad.

'Do you think she's going to come?' I asked Liz.

'Well, when I spoke to her she was already in the car and on her way,' she shrugged. 'We'll give her another fifteen minutes or so. I know this place can be tricky to find as it looks like a normal house.'

I was feeling quite nervous about meeting Mandy, even though Liz has asked me to sit in on the first contact session.

'Do you think she'll be OK with me being here?' I asked her.

'From what I've seen of her so far, she's a very gentle person so I don't think she'll give you any grief,' Liz told me. 'Plus I think it will be good for Mandy to meet you. You can answer any questions that she might have and she can pass on any info about the girls directly to you.

'Also, I think it will be a positive thing for the girls to see you chatting,' she continued.

I agreed with her. I always think it's nice when kids see their foster carer getting on with their birth parents. It stops them feeling guilty or that they have to take sides and it means they don't have to have divided loyalties.

A few minutes later, to my relief, we heard the front door slam shut.

'I bet that will be Mandy,' said Liz.

Sure enough, there was a buzz and a young woman walked through the double doors clutching a couple of carrier bags. Like her daughters, she was a big lady and she was out of breath.

'Hi, Mandy,' smiled Liz. 'Are you OK?'

'Hiya,' she puffed. 'Jim's just parking the car.'

She had a very youthful face with long, greasy brown hair and blue eyes like the girls. She had that same unhealthy look the girls had – her skin was pale, as though she hadn't seen much daylight. She was wearing a thick blue dress, but it was very old-fashioned and it looked like something a pensioner would wear, not a young woman in her early twenties.

'This is Maggie, the girl's foster carer,' Liz told her gently. 'I thought it would be nice if you got to meet her.'

I was always nervous about meeting birth parents as, under-standably, there was sometimes some animosity there. Their children had been taken away from them and I was the one looking after them. But Mandy seemed very friendly.

'Hiya,' she grinned. 'It took a long time to get here. We were in the car for ages. Is this your house?' she asked, looking around. 'It's really nice, isn't it? Very fancy.'

'Mandy, remember I explained the other day that you'd be meeting the girls at a contact centre?' Liz told her. 'This building isn't Maggie's house. It belongs to Social Services and it's a place where parents can spend time with their children.'

Just then, the double doors buzzed again and a man walked into the hallway. He was in his forties, tall and thin with long brown hair that was thinning on top. He looked a lot older than Mandy and smelt of sweat and cigarettes. He was wearing an old shirt and jeans and I noticed that his arms were covered in tattoos.

'Where are the girls?' he asked aggressively. 'Mand said they'd be here.'

Liz shot me a look.

'Jim, this is Maggie – the girls' foster carer,' she told him. 'Maggie, this is Mandy's brother Jim.'

'The girls are in a contact room with a member of staff,' Liz told him. 'I'm afraid we thought it would be good for just Mandy to see them on her own today, but perhaps we can arrange another session in the future where you can see them too?'

Jim shook his head.

'You never bloody told me that,' he snapped at Mandy. 'I'd have stayed at home and you could have got the bus.'

'Sorry,' sighed Mandy. 'I forgot.'

'She wouldn't even have come here today if I wasn't there to sort everything out and give her a lift,' he ranted to Liz. 'I'm not just a f***ing taxi service. I'm the girls' uncle, I deserve to see 'em too.'

'Of course,' nodded Liz. 'And we'd be happy to arrange that another time.'

'What am I supposed to do now then?' he sighed, looking annoyed. 'I guess I'll sit out here and have a cig.'

'I'm afraid there's no smoking on the premises,' Liz told him.

'I'll go and sit in the bloody car then,' he huffed.

'Ring me when you're out, will you?' he snapped at Mandy.

She shrugged, seeming unconcerned by his outrage.

'He ain't very happy, is he?' she giggled to me.

It was a relief when Jim left the building and we could get on with the session in peace. Billie and Bo were still with Janet in the contact room.

'Would you like to see the girls now?' Liz asked Mandy.

Mandy nodded eagerly.

As we pushed open the door, Billie and Bo both turned and looked up eagerly.

'Hiya, girls,' Mandy beamed.

They both heaved themselves up off the floor and waddled towards their mum as fast as their swollen legs would carry them. I couldn't help but smile, pleased that they were happy to see Mandy. As Billie launched herself towards her mum, I thought she was going to give her a cuddle, but instead, she snatched one of the carrier bags out of her hand. Bo grabbed the other one and they sat back down on the floor. Their faces lit up as they looked inside them.

Much to my surprise, they pulled out bags of Haribos, packets of biscuits, bars of chocolate and endless bags of crisps. The girls were like two hungry wolves as they frantically opened packet after packet and shoved the contents into their mouths as quickly as they could. It had all happened so fast that neither Liz or I had time to intervene.

'Aww, poor things must be really hungry,' giggled Mandy.

'Eat up, girls,' she told them as she lowered herself down on the floor next to them, ripping open a packet of biscuits.

I watched in dismay, my heart sinking. I'd been trying so hard these past few days to try and wean Billie and Bo off a constant diet of sugar, salt and fat and get them used to regular, balanced meals.

It never ceased to amaze me how much food parents will bring to contact sessions. Food is often used as a way of winning their child's affection – parents think that if they let their children eat all the treats they want or bring them loads of chocolate then they'll like them more or say they want to live with them. As a foster carer, I find it quite frustrating having to sit there and watch children overeat. They'll often come back to my house high on sugar and completely hyperactive. But as I watched Billie and Bo eat everything they could get their hands on, I knew it wasn't my place to say anything. I was there purely to observe. Janet had left when we'd come in, and Liz was the one running this session, but she didn't say anything.

Bo's face and hands were covered in chocolate by now and she snatched a packet of Monster Munch out of Billie's hands.

'Aw, Billie, do you want some more crispies?' Mandy asked her. 'I got some more. Monster Munch is her favourite,' she told us.

She started rummaging in her bag.

'Mandy, I think the girls have probably had enough to eat now,' Liz told her. 'We don't want them to be sick and Maggie will be making lunch for them later.'

Mandy laughed, dug a few more packets of crisps out of her bag and passed them to the girls.

'Ooh, she's being a meanie, ain't she?' she smiled. 'Quick, girls, eat 'em up whilst they're not looking.'

Liz and I exchanged a look of despair. I was shocked that Mandy thought it was acceptable for two young children to binge-eat their way through two big carrier bags of treats in one go.

'Mandy, I'll just go and pop these leftover packets in the kitchen so you can take them on the way out,' I told her.

I didn't want to risk the girls having any more to eat as I was worried they were going to be sick.

When I came back in, the girls were clambering all over Mandy. Bo was sitting on her legs and Billie was straddling her on her lap. Billie started tickling her mum and Mandy giggled and rolled back. All three of them squealed as they tipped over and started rolling round on the floor, tickling each other. It was like watching three kids playing and Mandy didn't appear to have any sense of embarrassment or self-consciousness as her legs swung up in the air and her dress rode up to reveal her knickers.

It was almost like they were wrestling with each other, and there was something about it that was uncomfortable to watch. I could see Liz felt the same way as she cleared her throat and said, 'Girls, why don't you show Mummy some of the games there are in the cupboard? That would be nice to all play a game together.'

'But we are playing a game,' said Billie. 'We're playing tickling.

'Mummy likes doing tickling.'

Tickling is an interesting subject for foster carers. In our training, we're taught not to tickle children. Tickling can be about power and control and the tickler is the one in charge. It makes the child feel powerless and they may not be able to say when they want it to stop. Tickling can also make kids lose control and it hypes them up. That was what was happening here, right in front of us. Mum was tickling them and the girls were getting more and more hyper and wound up. Bo looked like she was struggling to breathe.

I was glad when Liz stepped in and suggested the girls choose some toys out of the cupboard.

While the girls were busy playing with dolls, it gave me, Liz and Mandy time to have a chat.

'Is there is there anything you want to ask Maggie while she's here?' Liz asked her.

'Not really,' she shrugged.

Mandy seemed very sweet, but it was clear that she didn't understand the severity of the situation. She seemed very naïve and childlike.

'Is there anything you want to tell me about the girls or their routine?' I asked her. 'Is there anything they like doing or any particular food they like?'

She thought for a minute.

'Bo Bo loves Doritos and Billie likes her sweeties,' she smiled. 'They're good girls.'

'Mandy, we were hoping to get Billie a place in school,' Liz told her. 'Has she ever been to school before?'

Mandy shook her head.

'We ain't never had one near us and Jim said it was a waste of time,' she replied.

'Have you got one near you?' she asked me.

'There's a really lovely one just down the road,' I replied.

'It won't be for another week or so because we need to secure a place and sort out her uniform,' Liz told her.

Mandy suddenly started rummaging in her bag. She got out her purse and to my surprise, she pressed two pound coins into my hand.

'That's for the uniform,' she told me. 'Will that be enough?'

'You keep your money, Mandy,' Liz said gently. 'Social Services give Maggie a clothing allowance so she can get Billie's uniform out of that.'

'Oh, OK,' nodded Mandy.

For the first time since she'd arrived, she suddenly looked downcast.

'If you really wanted to get them something then I could keep the money and use it to buy some hair bobbles and slides for Bo and Billie from you?' I suggested. 'They can bring them in and show you what they've bought at the next contact?'

She nodded.

'I'd like that,' she smiled sadly. 'They've got lovely pretty hair.'

I felt sorry for Mandy. She seemed as much like a little girl as her two daughters.

Liz glanced up at the clock on the wall.

'I'm afraid our session is nearly over for today, Mandy,' she told her. 'Do you want to say goodbye to the girls?'

She looked confused.

'Aren't they coming back home now?' she asked. 'Aren't they allowed to come back with me and Jim?'

'Mandy, remember we spoke about this the other day,' Liz told her gently. 'We're going to see how things go. We need to talk to you and the girls and then we can see if they're able to come home, but it won't be today.'

Mandy still looked confused and what Liz was saying didn't seem to register, but she shrugged.

'Right, girls, I'm off,' she told them loudly. 'The lady says you ain't coming home today.'

'Can we have the sweets and crisps, Mummy?' asked Billie, looking unconcerned at her mum leaving.

Mandy grabbed some leftover packets from her bag and shoved them into Bo and Billie's hands.

'You can eat 'em when she isn't looking,' she grinned, gesturing to Liz.

The girls seemed more interested in ripping open the packets than saying goodbye to their mum.

I gently took the bags off them and said: 'Come on, let's say bye bye to Mummy properly.'

The girls waddled over to Mandy. Bo gave her a kiss on the lips and Billie did the same, but as Mandy kissed her on the lips, I noticed Billie stuck her tongue into her mum's mouth. It was just for a split second but I noticed it and I could see that Liz had too. It was all very odd behaviour.

'Come on, girls,' I told them. 'We need to tidy up these toys while Liz takes Mummy out.'

'Jim's waiting in the car, I best go now,' muttered Mandy, shuffling out.

The first thing I did was to clear up the leftover sweets and put them into a bag.

'Me want sweeties,' sighed Bo.

'You've had a lot of sweeties today, flower, so we'll save these for another time,' I told her.

'You're a meanie,' huffed Billie. 'They're ours.'

'You can still have them,' I told her. 'Just not any more today, or you'll give yourself a tummy ache.'

Sure enough, as we walked into the hallway at my house, Bo started crying.

'What is it, flower?' I asked her.

'Tummy hurts,' she wailed.

As if on cue, I suddenly saw brown liquid drip down her leg onto the floor.

'Oh, you poor thing,' I told her. 'Let's get you to the toilet and get that pull-up off and clean you up.'

Her upset stomach was probably a combination of nerves and feeling overwhelmed at seeing her mum, but mainly also because she'd had so many sweets, chocolates and crisps in such a short space of time. After a few days of good food, her digestive system was probably all over the place.

Liz rang me a couple of hour later.

'What did you make of Mum?' she asked me.

'I feel a bit sorry for her,' I sighed. 'She almost seems like a child herself, especially when she was tickling the girls and rolling round on the floor with them. And I have to say, that kiss goodbye at the end was a bit strange.'

'I think that was probably Billie just being silly,' Liz told me.

'You're probably right,' I said. 'Kids do daft things.'

Social Services were going to do a parenting assessment with Mandy to see whether she would be capable of looking after the girls again in the future.

'We need to know about where she's at,' Liz explained. 'We need to decide whether she can parent if we give her the help and support that she needs.'

It was early days and who knew what had been going on in their home behind closed doors? We didn't know enough about Mandy and her relationship with Billie and Bo, or even where Uncle Jim fitted in to all this. There were a lot of questions and, at this point in time, we didn't know the answers yet.

FIVE

Fading Away

'Oh, Billie,' I sighed as I saw the puddle by the patio doors.
'We do our wees in the toilet, remember?'

'What?' she asked, seemingly completely oblivious as she
played dolls with Bo.

Toilet training was in full swing, but getting a seven-year-
old who was used to going to the toilet wherever they wanted
was proving quite tricky. I'd decided to concentrate on Billie
first as she needed to be ready to start school and there was
no way I could send her until she'd got used to using the
toilet. For now, Bo was still in pull-ups so that I could focus
all my attention on getting Billie used to using the bathroom.

The thing that struck me was how unashamed Billie was
when she did it. She didn't care if anyone else was in the
room; she'd simply pull down her pants wherever she was
and without any embarrassment at all, she'd squat down and
do her business on the floor. This was obviously what she'd
always done at home so she couldn't understand why she
couldn't do that at my house.

I was using the same techniques that I used with any child, from toddler age upwards. I set a timer and, every twenty minutes, I took Billie to the toilet. With other children, sometimes I used treats as an incentive, but there was no way I was going to do that with Billie as I was still weaning the girls off their continual diet of crisps and sweets. Instead, we'd gone to Next and I'd got her to pick out some pants she liked. She'd chosen a pack with glittery unicorns on the front and was really excited at the prospect of wearing them.

'Remember those lovely unicorn pants we bought you?' I told her as I mopped up the puddle of urine. 'When you do your wees and poos in the toilet and not on the floor, you can wear them all the time.'

Just then there was a knock at the door. When I went to open it, to my surprise and delight, Louisa was standing there.

'Sorry, Maggie, you look like you're in the middle of something,' she told me as she saw the cleaning cloth and anti-bacterial spray in my hand. 'I just thought I'd pop round quickly after work and say hello to the girls.'

I'd called Louisa when Billie and Bo had first arrived and we'd texted a few times, but I hadn't seen her since they'd come to stay with me.

'What a treat to see you, lovey,' I smiled. 'You know you're always welcome here. Come on in.' I took her into the kitchen where the girls were playing.

'This is Bo and Billie,' I smiled. 'Girls, this is Louisa. She used to live with me a long time ago when she was little.'

Louisa was brilliant with children of all ages, and girls especially always warmed to her, drawn to her pretty hair and fashionable clothes, but despite her best efforts trying to chat to the girls, neither of them seemed particularly interested. I'd already told Louisa about their weight issues but I could see it was still a shock for her to see it herself.

'Gosh, those poor kids, Maggie, they're so big,' she whispered to me. 'They should be running round at that age, but they can hardly even walk.'

'I know,' I nodded.

Just then the timer on my phone went off, and it was time to take Billie to the toilet again. We were only a few days into toilet training and Billie already looked a little bit fed up of it all.

'Mummy didn't make me do this at my house,' she puffed as I marched her to the toilet.

I knew it was important not to shame Mandy or put her down in front of Billie, but I wanted her to realise we did things a little differently from what she was familiar with.

'Lots of things are different at this house,' I told her. 'We have meals sitting at the table together, we brush our teeth twice a day and we do our wees and poos in the toilet. That way, we don't have to spend all our time cleaning up and we can do other, more fun things.'

I also used school as an incentive for Billie.

'As soon as you remember to use the toilet, you can go to school,' I told her. 'You'll need a pencil case and new shoes and you'll wear a special jumper with a big badge on it. You'll meet lots of children your age and you'll get to make lots of friends. Does that sound exciting?'

She nodded, and I was hopeful that at last she was taking it all in. Louisa and I managed a quick cup of tea and a catch up, but ten minutes later, I walked into the hall to find a poo outside the living-room door. It was late afternoon and this was the fifth accident of the day.

'Oh, Billie,' I sighed.

I wasn't angry. I knew it wasn't her fault, I was just weary.

'Billie, come and help me clean up,' I asked her gently.

'I'm playing,' she shouted back crossly.

'No, Billie, I'm afraid you need to go and get the the wipes for me whilst I get the mop and bucket, and then come into the hall and help me clean up the mess,' I told her. 'If you did your poos in the toilet, then you could carry on playing.'

I wanted to make her realise that when she did this, someone else was having to clean it up. It was about showing her that there were consequences to her actions.

Reluctantly, she trudged through with me to get the wipes.

'Listen, you look like you've got your hands full, Maggie so I'll leave you to it,' Louisa told me. 'Charlie will be home soon, so I'll head back.'

'You don't fancy bleaching the floor for me?' I joked.

'I'll stay if you want me to help,' she replied, concerned.

'Don't be daft, lovey, I was only joking,' I told her. 'You need to look after yourself and that baby.'

I said goodbye to Louisa and then got on with cleaning the floor. Just as I'd finished, my mobile rang.

It was Zoe – one of the carers who looked after Natalie's nan Peggy. Natalie had been to visit her after school tonight.

'Nat's just left and I wanted to let you know that she might be a bit upset when she comes back,' she told me. 'Peggy's not had a great day.

'She had a choking fit and we had to manually help her clear her chest and I think it was very distressing for Nat to see.'

'Oh no,' I sighed. 'I'm so sorry to hear that. Poor Nat.'

I knew from what Natalie had said recently that Peggy was deteriorating rapidly.

'Thank you for letting me know,' I told Zoe.

As if on cue, a few seconds later I heard a key in the front door and Natalie walked into the hallway.

'How are you, flower?' I asked her gently.

I could already see for myself. Her eyes were bloodshot and I could tell she'd been crying.

'Oh, lovey,' I sighed, pulling her into a hug. 'Zoe just rang and said things weren't great with your Nan today.'

It didn't take much for the tears to start flowing again.

'It was horrible, Maggie,' she sobbed. 'She couldn't breathe. She was choking and I couldn't help her.'

'I'm so sorry,' I told her, giving her a squeeze. 'That must have been so upsetting for you to watch. Do you want to come into the kitchen and say hello to the girls and I'll make you a drink?'

She shook her head.

'I'm just gonna go to my room for a bit,' she told me before she headed upstairs. I knew better than to push her, and knew it was best to give her some time to process what had happened that day. Nat adored her nan, and I could only imagine how difficult it was for her to see her suffering so badly.

Eventually Natalie came back downstairs, but for the rest of the evening she was very quiet. Billie and Bo kept me busy and it wasn't until they'd had a bath and gone to bed that we finally had time to chat. I didn't want to push her to talk because she looked drained, but I needed to make sure that she was OK.

'It must have been so hard for you today to see your nan like that,' I told her gently once we were both sitting in the living room together. 'If it's making you upset or distressed then you don't have to visit her three times a week any more if you don't want to. You could just go once or twice, perhaps, or not at all if you don't feel up to it.'

Nat was very mature for her age, but at just eleven years old, I knew it was a lot for her to cope with.

Natalie nodded.

'I know,' she sighed. 'She doesn't talk any more and she sleeps a lot but she's still my nan and I want to see her.'

'Well, how about the next time you go, I come with you and keep you company?' I suggested.

'Yeah,' she nodded. 'Nan really likes you, Maggie. I think she'd like that.'

I'd met Peggy several times since Natalie had come into care. Sometimes when I went to pick Nat up, I'd popped in to say hello to Peggy, but I hadn't seen her for months.

'But what about Billie and Bo?' she asked. 'Will they have to come too?'

'I could ask Louisa to look after them,' I told her. 'It would only be for an hour or so.'

Billie and Bo were taking up a lot of my attention at the moment, but Natalie still needed my support too, and at a time like this, I knew her needs had to take priority, and I was sure Louisa wouldn't mind. I could have asked my friends Carol and Vicky who were both foster carers, but they had their own foster children to take care of so it was easier for Louisa to pop round. She was DBS checked because of her nannying job and she'd met the girls before when she'd popped in.

Nat seemed relieved, and I was glad I was able to do something small to make all this a little easier for her.

As time passed, Billie and Bo gradually seemed to be a bit more settled. They'd been with me for a couple of weeks now, and I was keeping things very quiet and simple. We spent our days at home, trying to crack toilet training and getting them used to three balanced meals a day. There were still incessant demands for snacks and sweets but I was trying to give them healthier snacks like fruit and rice cakes. I also made sure we got out for a walk each day even if it was just to the local shops to get milk or bread.

They were still having contact twice a week with Mandy, and both girls seemed to enjoy seeing their mum. I no longer attended the sessions, but Liz had informed me that Mandy had continued bringing bags of food with her each time, and Liz had been forced to have a word with her. The girls were usually exhausted after their contact sessions, and I tried to keep things as calm as possible for them in between.

Three days later, Louisa came round. It was her day off from her nannying job so she was able to look after the girls for me. I was meeting Natalie after school and going round to Peggy's house with her.

'OK, girls. Louisa's going to look after you for a bit because I've just got to pop out with Natalie,' I told them. 'I'll be back soon.'

'Who's going to do tea time?' asked Billie, a concerned look on her face. I was pleased to see that she was getting used to the structure of our days, and I knew that any disruption to her usual schedule might upset her.

'Me and Nat will be back by then, sweetie, and we'll all have tea together, but if anything happens to make us late then Louisa will give you some tea,' I reassured her.

I warned Louisa that we were still persevering with the toilet training. I talked her through setting the timer for every twenty minutes and taking Billie to the toilet.

'She's slowly getting the hang of it,' I told her. 'It's just getting her out of old habits and reminding her.'

'Oh God, I don't think I can handle it if she does a big poo on the floor, Maggie,' shuddered Louisa. 'I don't know how you do it. I can cope when it's a toddler but not a seven-year-old.'

To be honest, cleaning up poo wasn't nice but it didn't really bother me too much. For me, the most difficult thing was if kids were sick, as I found it really hard to deal with vomit. I'd been known to throw bedding away rather than wash it if it was covered in sick.

'Well, hopefully she won't,' I reassured her. 'She's gradually getting into the swing of things.'

It felt strange being without the girls as we'd been together all day every day for so long. I trusted Louisa completely though. She was more than capable and I knew she'd be fine.

I parked up near Natalie's school and waited for her so we could walk the five minutes to Peggy's flat together.

'Nan might look a bit different from since you saw her last time,' Natalie explained. 'When she tries to talk, she just makes a noise like a robot and she has this funny mask over her face to help her breathe.

'But it's still Nan.'

'Gosh, that must be so hard for you to see,' I told her. 'Thank you for telling me.'

Bless her, she was trying to prepare me. Natalie was such a kind, sensible young girl, and my heart went out to her for having to deal with so much at such a young age.

But despite Nat's warning, nothing could prepare me for how Peggy looked now. The last time I'd seen her, three months ago, she'd been tired but she could still talk, sitting up in her wheelchair and laughing with Nat, though at times it could be hard to understand what she was saying. Now, she had a special bed set up downstairs in the front room of her house and she looked so tiny in it. Her skin looked grey and she had a mask over her face attached to a ventilator and an IV drip giving her pain relief. It was heartbreaking to see a woman who had once been so full of life looking so frail and vulnerable, and she looked much, much older than her sixty-five years.

I wanted to cry for Natalie and how it must feel for her, seeing her beloved nan suffering so much. The nurse who had called in from the palliative-care team was really kind and friendly, as were Peggy's carers, and they gave us some space as we sat in a couple of chairs by Peggy's bed.

'Hello, Peggy,' I smiled, though I knew she couldn't respond. 'It's lovely to see you again. Isn't Natalie getting grown up these days?'

Peggy didn't respond, but Nat stroked her hand gently.

'I can make us all a cup of tea if you want?' suggested Natalie.

'That would be lovely, Nat,' I smiled.

This house was where she'd lived for pretty much most of her life, and although she'd been with me for over a year, it was still her home.

Zoe, the carer who I'd spoken to on the phone the other day, came and sat with me once Nat had pottered out into the kitchen.

'Bless her,' she sighed. 'She's such a lovely girl and I can see how much she loves her nan. It's a lot for her to cope with.'

'How is she doing?' I asked quietly, gesturing to Peggy.

'She's on constant pain relief now, which makes her sleep a lot, and her breathing muscles are gradually weakening,' she told me. 'I'm afraid she hasn't got long left.'

'Weeks?' I asked.

She sighed.

'She's deteriorating so quickly now, it may even be days, I'm afraid. It's such a vicious disease.'

My heart broke for Natalie upon hearing the news. I knew her nan was her world. Nat's mum had never been reliable, as she'd struggled with addiction from before Nat was born. Nat had never had her dad around in her life, and as an only child, Peggy *was* her family.

We stayed a little longer, making small talk, but it was clear that Nat was exhausted and finding it difficult seeing her nan looking so poorly.

I left that night with a sinking feeling in my stomach. I didn't know if Natalie realised how sick Peggy was. Nat knew that Peggy had a disease that would eventually kill her but she'd been ill for so long and I wasn't sure if Nat realised that her death was imminent. I'd always been open and honest with her and I felt like I owed it to her to prepare her.

'How do you think your nan's doing?' I asked her in the car on the way home.

She shrugged.

'Not very good,' she sighed. 'She sleeps all the time, she can't talk and she needs that funny mask to breathe.'

She paused.

'Do you think she's going to die soon, Maggie?'

It was a question that I didn't want to answer but I knew I had to. I took a deep breath and swallowed the lump in my throat.

'I'm so sorry, flower, but I think she might,' I told her gently.

She stared out of the car window.

'Will she have to go into hospital?' she asked.

'As long as she's comfortable and not in any pain then I think the nurses will try and keep her at home,' I told her. 'That's what your nan said she wanted.'

Natalie nodded.

'Will dying hurt her?'

'The nurses will make sure she's not in any pain,' I reassured her. 'One day she'll probably just fall asleep and not wake up again.'

Natalie stared out of the window and I saw a tear roll down her cheek.

'I'm so sorry, Nat,' I told her. 'I can only imagine how hard all this is for you. I know how much you love Peggy.'

'What she's like now isn't really my nan,' she sighed. 'I miss her so much, Maggie. We used to have so much fun together and now she just lies there all the time. I don't even know if she understands what I'm saying to her.'

I knew there was nothing I could say or do to make this any better and I felt really helpless. All I could do was be there for Nat, and make clear to her that she wasn't alone.

As we pulled up outside the house, my thoughts turned back to Billie and Bo for the first time since we'd arrived at Peggy's. I hoped Louisa had managed OK and there were no disasters waiting for me.

As we walked in the front door, I was relieved to see that everything looked calm enough. The girls were watching TV in the living room and waved mutely at me when I went in to say hello. Nat went upstairs to her bedroom and I went into the kitchen with Louisa.

'How have they been?' I asked her. 'Any accidents?'

'No accidents,' she replied, her voice sounding a little strained. 'Although we did have an incident, Maggie.'

'What sort of incident?' I asked, concerned.

I listened as she explained the girls had been playing Barbies in the living room.

'I left them for a couple of minutes while I went to get them a drink of water from the kitchen,' she told me. 'And when I got back Billie was . . . um . . .' She hesitated. 'I'm not sure how to say this.'

'What was Billie doing, lovey?' I asked.

'It sounds really weird, but Billie had pulled Bo's pants down and was trying to shove the Barbie between her legs.'

'What?' I gasped.

'When I asked her what she was doing she said she was putting it in Bo's noo noo.' Louisa looked deeply troubled, and my heart sank upon hearing what had happened.

'What did you do?'

'Well, I just said we don't play with Barbies like that, then I distracted her with some other toys and gave the Barbie a good scrub with hot water,' she told me.

'And how was Bo?'

'She didn't seem bothered or upset in the slightest, and she wasn't hurt,' shrugged Louisa. 'It's a bit strange for a seven-year-old to do that though, isn't it, Maggie?'

'It is odd,' I said, frowning.

I suddenly remembered that she'd tried to do a similar thing with a bath toy when the girls had first arrived.

'Why do you think she was doing it?' asked Louisa.

'Remember, Billie's toilet training at the minute and kids often get very hung up and fixated on their private parts when that happens,' I told her. 'I also think Billie's immature for her age and you know how toddlers get obsessed by boobs and bums and willies. She's talked about noo noos a couple of times before.'

Whatever the reasons behind Billie's actions, it was certainly odd behaviour that I needed to keep an eye on, for both of the girls' sakes. I also needed to make a note of it in my daily recordings that I emailed to Liz and Becky every evening.

That night, I couldn't get to sleep. I tossed and turned all night, as I lay there thinking about Natalie and poor Peggy and everything that she was going through and worrying about how Billie and Bo were doing.

I was still bleary-eyed the next morning when my mobile rang. It was Jenny, Natalie's social worker. Nat's old social worker had left a few months ago and I didn't know Jenny all that well.

My heart was in my throat as I answered, and I immediately feared the worst.

'I'm ringing to let you know that unfortunately Peggy's taken a turn for the worse overnight,' Jenny explained. 'I wanted to let Natalie know and also to tell her that her aunt is coming down to see Peggy.'

'I'll tell Nat,' I replied. 'We went to see Peggy yesterday and it was clear that she was deteriorating.'

'It might be worth giving Natalie the option to go and visit her nan again today if she wants?' Jenny suggested. 'I can let school know the situation.'

'OK, thanks,' I told her.

When Natalie got up, I went and had a word with her in her bedroom before Billie and Bo woke up.

'Jenny just called to say your aunt is coming down today to see your nan,' I told her.

Her face lit up.

'Oh, is Auntie Tina bringing my cousins?' she asked.

'No, flower,' I replied. 'Peggy's really poorly now so your auntie is just coming on her own so that she can spend some time with her.'

I could see the realisation dawn on Nat's face as to why her aunt was suddenly visiting out of the blue.

Tina lived hundreds of miles away in Scotland. I'd met her once when she'd visited and Nat had gone to stay with her a couple of times in the school holidays for a few days. When Peggy had first got ill, Tina had suggested that Natalie go and live with her, but Natalie was settled at school and she wanted to stay in the local area so she could still see Peggy whenever she wanted.

'Jenny thought you might want you to go and see your nan today as well,' I told her. 'I can ring school if you want to go this morning?'

'But we only went to see her last night,' she replied, looking confused. 'I've got drama at school today and I can't miss that.'

'Nat, I really think it would be a good idea,' I urged her gently. 'The nurses have said Peggy is really poorly.'

'OK,' she nodded, realisation dawning, and I could see the fear in her eyes. It was so hard knowing there was nothing I could do to alleviate the pain she was experiencing.

I rang Jenny back and told her what was happening and she offered to pick Natalie up and take her to Peggy's, which was a relief, as I didn't have anyone to look after Billie and Bo.

'I'll be thinking of you today, lovey,' I told her, giving her hand a squeeze. 'And it will be nice to have your auntie with you.'

She nodded.

I gave Jenny a wave out of the window and watched with a heavy heart as they drove off down the street.

I tried to focus on Billie and Bo and kept them entertained with an arts and crafts project, but Natalie was on my mind all day, and I couldn't help but worry about what might be happening.

Jenny had said she'd let me know when she was bringing Natalie back, but I didn't hear anything until later that afternoon when my phone rang.

'Hi Maggie, it's Natalie's aunt, Tina,' said a Scottish accent on the end of the line. 'Is it all right if she stays later tonight?'

'Of course it is,' I told her. 'She can stay as long as she needs to. How are things there?'

'Not good,' she said, her voice choking up. 'But at least Mum's comfortable.'

'I'm so sorry, Tina. Let me know if there's anything at all I can do,' I told her.

'Thank you,' she told me. 'It's just a waiting game.'

But over the next few hours, as I gave Billie and Bo dinner and a bath and got them to bed, there was still no word.

By the time I flopped down on the sofa, after sorting out some washing and tidying up the kitchen, it was gone 9 p.m. I still hadn't heard anything more from Tina or Natalie. I turned on the telly but I couldn't concentrate on anything. I wasn't a religious person but I closed my eyes and I said a prayer. I prayed for Natalie and Tina and I prayed for Peggy. I wasn't Natalie's mother, but over the past year that she'd been with me, she'd become part of my family and my heart ached for all that she had been through and what she was about to face.

I must have fallen asleep on the sofa because I was woken up by a gentle tapping on the front door. Groggily, I sat myself up and looked at my watch – it was almost midnight.

I went to the front door and opened it to find Tina and Natalie standing there. They both looked exhausted and Natalie's face was streaked with tears.

'Mum passed away a couple of hours ago,' whispered Tina.

'Oh, lovey,' I sighed. 'I'm so sorry.'

Natalie's face crumpled and she collapsed into my arms, sobbing.

SIX

Life and Loss

I managed to guide Natalie into the kitchen and sit her down.

She was utterly distraught.

'I can't believe she's gone,' she sobbed.

Tina, in comparison, seemed shell-shocked and was very quiet.

'It's been such a long day and you must both be so tired,' I soothed. 'Can I get you a drink or something to eat?'

'I'm not hungry,' Nat said shakily. 'I feel really sick.'

'The nurses were really kind and made us a sandwich but neither of us could manage anything,' sighed Tina.

'Well, let me know if you change your mind,' I told them.

I was at a loss to know what to say or do to help them.

'I'm so sorry about Peggy,' I said gently. 'She was such a lovely lady and I know how much she meant to you both.'

'Thank you,' replied Tina. 'It doesn't seem real at the minute. I just feel numb.'

She walked over to Natalie and put her arms around her.

'Natalie, love, I'm going to go back to my hotel now and try and get some sleep,' she told her. 'But I'll come back in the morning and we'll go round to Nan's, OK?'

Nat looked up at her with red raw eyes and nodded.

'I'm shattered but I'm not sure I can sleep,' Tina told me.

'I'd love to be able to invite you to stay here but as I've got other foster children I'm afraid I'm not allowed to without you having all the relevant checks,' I explained.

'Don't worry, I understand,' she said, smiling sadly. 'Child protection rules are there for a reason.

'I'll see you in the morning, pet,' she told Natalie.

Natalie let out a gut-wrenching sob and Tina gave her another hug.

'It's going to be OK,' she soothed. 'I'll come round and see you tomorrow.'

Natalie nodded bravely. After I'd walked Tina to the door, I went back into the kitchen.

'You should try and get some sleep too, lovey,' I told Nat gently. 'It's late and you've had such a tough day,'

'I'm not tired,' she sighed. 'I just keep thinking about Nan.'

'I know it's late, but how about I run you a nice bath?' I suggested. 'That might help relax you.'

While Natalie was in the bath, I emailed her social worker Jenny and my supervising social worker Becky to let them know that Peggy had died. Then afterwards, when Natalie was in her pyjamas, I took her up a steaming mug of hot chocolate and a couple of slices of toast.

'Thanks, Maggie, but I don't feel like it,' she sighed.

'Just try at least to have a couple of mouthfuls,' I told her. It will make you feel better.'

But she took a little nibble and pushed the plate away.

She curled up on her bed and I sat down at the end and stroked her long dark hair.

'Where do you go to when you die, Maggie?' she asked me in a quiet voice.

'I honestly don't know, flower,' I told her. 'No one truly knows what happens when you die. But knowing Peggy and how much she loved you, I bet she's out there somewhere watching over you, being as proud as she always was.'

'Do you really think she was proud of me?' asked Natalie.

'Of course she was,' I told her. 'You meant the world to her and everyone could see how much she loved you. You're a brilliant girl, Nat, and you meant the world to your nan. Even though she's gone, you'll always carry that love with you for ever.'

Natalie's eyes filled up with tears again.

'You were right about dying, Maggie,' she sighed. 'It wasn't scary and I don't think it hurt her.'

She tearfully explained how they'd held Peggy's hands and the nurses had encouraged them to talk to her.

'I don't know if she could hear us or not,' sighed Nat. 'Then she did lots of funny breathing and that was it, the nurse said she was gone.'

'That sounds really lovely and peaceful,' I told her gently. 'I bet your nan was so glad that you and Tina were there.'

I could feel myself getting upset now and I had to fight to hold back my own tears.

'It feels like a bad dream,' she stuttered, welling up again. 'I wish I could wake up in the morning and it had never happened.'

'I know, flower,' I sighed. 'I wish that too. But it's really important now that you try and get some sleep.'

I tucked her into bed and she insisted that I left the bedside lamp on.

'Will you stay with me, Maggie, till I fall asleep?' she asked.

'Of course I will, lovey,' I said.

It was important that Natalie knew I was there for her. I went and got my book and sat on the rocking chair in the corner of the bedroom.

'You close your eyes and I'll be right here,' I whispered.

But my head was too full and my heart was too heavy to read. Poor Natalie kept tossing and turning and she was so unsettled, shifting around in her bed.

Then finally she was still and ten minutes later, I heard her gentle little snores. I walked over and lightly kissed the top of her head.

Even though she knew it was going to happen one day, it was so hard for Nat to lose Peggy. She'd been rejected by her birth mother and her nan had always been there for her.

Back in my own bedroom, I finally let out the tears that I'd been holding in since Natalie had got home. I was shattered too by now, but I couldn't sleep. All I could think about was Natalie. I knew she was restless as I heard her get up a couple of times in the night to go to the toilet.

I was still lying there with my eyes wide open as it got light.

I quietly looked in on Natalie and thankfully she was finally in a deep sleep. I let her sleep in while I got Billie and Bo up. I didn't mention anything to the girls as they were too young to understand, but I rang Natalie's school to tell them what had happened and that she wouldn't be in for the next few days.

She finally came downstairs around 10 a.m. Her eyes were bloodshot and puffy and I could see she'd been crying again.

'How are you feeling, lovey?' I asked, putting my arm around her.

She shrugged and wiped away her tears.

'Try and have a little bit of breakfast,' I told her, putting some cereal boxes down in front of her, but she just pushed them away.

'I feel sick,' she said.

'Your auntie just called,' I told her. 'She's going to come round and pick you up in an hour. I think she's meeting the funeral director at Peggy's house.'

Tina wanted Natalie to be involved in the service and help pick her nan's favourite songs.

'What's a funeral director?' she asked.

'When someone dies, everyone who knew and loved them gets together and you have some sort of a service to remember them by,' I explained.

'The funeral director is the person who helps you organise it all. Have you ever been to a funeral before?' I asked her and she shook her head.

'You don't have to go to your nan's house today if you don't want,' I told her. 'You can stay here if you'd prefer?'

Funeral arrangements were probably very boring for an eleven-year-old and I was conscious that it was a lot for her to cope with.

'I want to go,' she said firmly. 'I want to help Auntie Tina.'

When Tina arrived, she looked like she'd had a sleepless night too.

'Bring her back any time,' I told her. 'I'll make sure I'm at home.'

That morning, I took Billie and Bo out for a quick walk in the park. We all needed some fresh air and exercise and I wanted to clear my head. After a few weeks with me, they were much more comfortable walking than they had been, and it was a relief to be out in the bright sunshine after a long, dark night.

While the girls were playing, I made a few phone calls. I rang Becky as I hadn't spoken to her since I'd emailed her last night.

'Poor Natalie,' she sighed. 'How's she doing?'

'As you can imagine, she's devastated,' I told her.

'Give her my love and tell her how sorry I am,' Becky said.

I also left a message for Louisa and called Graham. I hadn't seen him since our lunch a few weeks ago, although we'd managed the odd phone call. He didn't know Natalie well but he was really sad to hear the news.

'Let me know if there's anything I can do to help, Maggie,' he told me.

I didn't know what he could do. To be honest, I didn't even know what I could do. I thought back on the things that had helped Louisa all those years ago after her parents had died, as well as reflecting on the other bereaved children I'd fostered over the years. I knew that all I could really do was to be there for Natalie, encourage her to talk about her nan if she wanted and offer her a hug when she needed one.

I decided the best thing to do was to try and keep everything as normal as possible at home. She spent the next few days planning Peggy's funeral with Tina. They picked Peggy's favourite songs and ordered her favourite spring flowers, daffodils and tulips.

When Tina dropped Natalie off one afternoon, I invited her in for a coffee. The girls were watching TV in the living room while we went into the kitchen and I put the kettle on.

'I wanted to have a chat to you actually,' Tina told me. 'I talked to Jenny, Nat's social worker, today.

'She came round to the house to see how Nat was doing. I asked her what I needed to do to get the ball rolling for Nat to come and live with me.'

'Oh,' I stuttered, taken aback. 'Is that something that you want to do?'

'It's something I've always wanted, but it just wasn't what Natalie or Mum wanted when she first got ill.

'Nat didn't want to move to Scotland then because she didn't want to have to change schools and she wanted to be near Mum and be able to see her. I know that was important for Mum too, so the timing wasn't right.

'But now Mum's gone, I would love it if Nat would come and live with us.'

'Have you talked about it with Nat?' I asked.

'Yes, we had a chat about it today,' Tina told me. 'I was worried it would be too much, too soon, but she seemed really keen.

'My sister was never there for her but I want to be. My husband Don is all for it and I know my girls would be thrilled.'

Tina had two daughters who were six and nine.

It was a bit of shock for me – I'd been fostering Nat for over a year now, and she meant the world to me, but in my heart of hearts I knew it would be in her best interests to be with her family. Scotland was such a long way away, but now that Peggy had died there was nothing keeping her here any more. Maybe a fresh start was what she needed?

'I've always said to Nat that she can say with me for as long as she wants to,' I told her. 'She knows I'm very fond of her. But as long as she's happy, I'm happy.'

'Great,' smiled Tina. 'Jenny's going to start the process off.'

Just as I took a swig of coffee, Natalie came running into the kitchen.

'Maggie, can you please come and tell Billie to stop,' she sighed.

'What's she doing?' I asked, jumping up.

'She's moaning and groaning and fiddling with herself,' she told us, looking horrified. 'You know, touching herself down there.'

Tina and I looked at each other in shock. I went into the living room where Bo and Billie were sitting next to each other on the sofa. Bo was glued to the television, seemingly oblivious to what was happening around her. Billie was sitting beside her sister, but she had her hands down her pants, her eyes were closed and she was writhing around.

'Billie, stop doing that,' hissed Natalie. 'It's disgusting. Maggie, tell her.'

Normally, it was toddlers who had their hands constantly down their pants, but Billie was seven and it wasn't really appropriate to be doing this in front of other people. It was a tricky situation. I wasn't going to tell her off for exploring her body. I didn't want her to think it was something shameful but she needed to know what was and wasn't appropriate.

'Come on, Billie, love, let's go to the toilet and wash your hands,' I told her.

Distraction was always the best technique. She heaved herself up of the sofa and slowly followed me to the downstairs toilet.

'Sweetie, we don't put our hands down our pants in front of other people,' I told her gently. 'There's nothing wrong with touching our bodies but we do it in private.'

'I was only playing,' she sighed.

'I know you were, lovey, but I'm afraid it's not OK to play like that in front of other people.'

Billie nodded, and once she'd washed and dried her hands, she settled back on the sofa next to her sister, seemingly content to watch the programme.

'Sorry about that,' I told Tina as I went back into the kitchen.

I quickly steered the conversation away from Billie and back to Natalie going to live with her.

'I know Social Services will need to do lots of checks but I'm prepared to wait,' she told me.

'If Jenny doesn't have any concerns then it shouldn't really take that long,' I replied. 'There will have to be some basic checks, but with kinship care, which is what we call it when a child goes to live with another family member, the system's designed to be fairly quick.'

'That's great,' smiled Tina.

That night, after I'd put the girls to bed, I went downstairs and sat with Natalie on the sofa. She snuggled into me and I put my arm around her.

She wasn't normally a hugely affectionate girl but in the past few days since Peggy had died she'd been very clingy.

'How are you feeling, flower?' I asked her.

'OK,' she said bravely, but I could tell that she wasn't

'Your Auntie Tina was saying that she'd talked to you about going to live with her,' I told her. 'How do you feel about that?'

'I know Scotland's a long way and it doesn't mean I don't like it here, but she's the only family I've got left,' she told me.

'I understand that, lovey. Does that mean you'd like to go then?' I asked and she nodded.

'Do you think Jenny will let me?'

'If you want to go then I think she will, yes,' I told her, smiling.

'I'll miss you, you know,' she added.

'And I'll miss you too,' I told her. 'I care for you enormously and you'll always have a home here if you want one, but it's so nice for you to be able to be with your auntie and uncle and cousins.'

The next day, Jenny called me to discuss it.

'What do you think about it, Maggie?' she asked. 'According to Natalie's file, we had looked at this originally when Peggy first got ill but at the time Natalie didn't want to move far away from Peggy.'

'I talked to Nat and she seems happy with it,' I told her.

'Do you think it could be too soon?' asked Jenny.

'No, I think she would cope,' I replied. 'She's been through a lot, but she's a tough little thing and I can tell that she really loves her aunt.'

As I put the phone down, the reality hit me. Natalie could be leaving in a matter of weeks.

That evening, Louisa and Charlie were coming round for tea. We'd arranged it before Peggy had died.

'We can come another time if you think it will be too much for Nat?' asked Louisa when she phoned that afternoon.

'No, I think it will be fine,' I told her. 'It will cheer her up. Nat loves you.'

In fact, her face lit up when I told Nat that Louisa was coming, and when they arrived, she ran to the door and gave her a hug.

Although she still didn't like talking about it, Louisa had quite a noticeable little bump now.

'Gosh you've really popped out in the past few days,' I smiled as we all sat down in the living room. 'There's no mistaking there's a baby in there.'

Louisa blushed, but I was pleased to see a tiny smile on her face as she patted her little bump proudly.

Billie was listening to the conversation and suddenly her face lit up. She got up and went over to Charlie and tapped him on the arm.

'I know what you did,' she told him shyly.

'What's that?' he smiled.

'You stuck your willy in her noo noo and it did that,' she said matter-of-factly, pointing to Louisa's stomach.

The room suddenly went deathly quiet. Louisa looked shocked and Charlie's mouth opened and closed like a goldfish. Bo was completely oblivious to what had been said but Natalie burst out laughing.

'She said noo noo,' she sniggered.

I did the only thing I could think of.

'Would anyone like a cup of tea?' I asked cheerily, changing the subject as quickly as I could.

As I hurried into the kitchen and busied myself with putting the kettle on, I couldn't get rid of this growing sense that something wasn't right with Billie and her overly sexual behaviour. Where had she got this from? It wasn't as if she had ever gone to school or mixed with a lot of other children. I knew it was something that Liz and I needed to talk about in more detail, sooner rather than later.

Thankfully, the rest of the evening passed without any more incidents or drama, and we all had a nice dinner together.

'Will you do a plait in my hair, Louisa?' Natalie asked Louisa after dinner. Unlike me, Louisa was a dab hand at doing all sorts of fancy hair styles, and Nat loved playing around with hair and make-up.

'Can you do me one too?' asked Billie shyly.

'Of course I can,' smiled Louisa.

While Charlie helped me clear away the dishes in the kitchen, Louisa's hair salon opened up for business in the living room. Ten minutes later, I went in to see how they were getting on.

Billie was sitting on the sofa while Louisa sat behind her, braiding her long dark hair. Natalie and Bo were sitting on the floor together, watching.

'Do you like my hair, Maggie?' Nat asked, showing me the intricate French plait that Louisa had done.

'It looks lovely,' I told her.

It was nice to see Nat smiling for the first time in a few days.

'Me want one,' shouted Bo. 'Me want one.'

'You can have one too if you want,' Louisa smiled. 'As soon as I've finished your sister's hair, then I'll do yours.'

Bo clapped her hands excitedly and I was so grateful to Louisa for this little pocket of calm. I knew this was what Billie and Bo needed more than anything – a normal, stable family life, free from any drama.

Long may it continue, I thought to myself.

SEVEN

Endings and Beginnings

Despite her grief, I knew what Natalie needed more than anything was some security and routine. After a few days, Tina went back to Scotland and I thought Natalie could do with some normality too.

'I think you need to go back to school now, flower,' I told her gently. 'I know you're still dreadfully upset but I think it would be good for you to see your friends and get back to your lessons.'

'Do I have to?' she sighed. 'What about Nan's funeral?'

'You can have some more time off around the funeral and when Tina comes back down,' I replied. 'Your pastoral care worker knows what's happened so you can always go and talk to her if you're having a bad day or you need a bit of extra support. I know it feels really hard going back, lovey, but I really do think it will help you.'

I hoped that being back at school would provide her with a bit of a distraction, rather than sitting around at home with me, Billie and Bo.

In the meantime, Nat's social worker Jenny was starting the process of looking at whether Natalie could go and live with her aunt permanently. This week, she was going to travel up to Scotland to visit Tina at home and meet her husband and children to check everything seemed OK.

'It all feels like it's moving so fast,' I confided in Louisa when she popped in one night after Billie and Bo were in bed, and Nat was watching TV.

'I can't believe Nat's leaving,' she sighed.

'It won't be until after the funeral at least, and Tina is going to come down again in a few days and sort out Peggy's house as they've given notice to the housing association.'

I suddenly noticed Louisa shifting in her chair and wincing.

'Are you OK, lovey?' I asked her, suddenly aware that we hadn't talked much about her.

'Oh, I'm fine,' she shrugged. 'I've just got a bit of a bad back at the minute.'

She paused.

'I've got my scan next week,' she told me in a quiet voice.

I knew her twenty-week scan was something Louisa was dreading. It was at that scan that she'd found out there was something wrong with Dominic and been told that he wasn't likely to live.

'Oh, Louisa,' I sighed. 'It will be OK this time. I know it will.'

'How do you know though, Maggie?' she asked, suddenly sounding very young and afraid. 'No one can say that one hundred per cent.'

I knew she was right, but everything *had* to be OK with this baby.

'Do you want me to come to the hospital with you for moral support?' I asked her, desperate to help in any way that I could.

'Thanks, Maggie. I really appreciate it, but Charlie's going to have the day off so we'll be OK,' she told me.

I could see she was putting on a brave face. I hoped that if this scan went OK, Louisa would allow herself to relax a little bit and enjoy the rest of her pregnancy. Normally, I'd be knitting cardigans and hats and shopping for baby things by now, but after the trauma of losing baby Dominic, I just couldn't bring myself to do any of it this time around for fear of jinxing something.

'Anyway, let's not talk any more about that,' she said, quickly changing the subject. 'How are Bo and Billie doing?'

'They're OK,' I told her. 'Billie has finally cracked the toilet training so tomorrow we're going to go and look round the local school.'

As far as we knew, she'd never had any formal education, so I was hoping that she would settle OK.

'I'm quite looking forward to spending some time with just Bo,' I went on. 'Billie is definitely the dominant one and Bo doesn't get a look in when she's around.'

I didn't feel like I really knew Bo yet. In the past three weeks, her speech had come on in leaps and bounds and she was saying a lot more.

'Well, I hope it goes OK,' Louisa told me. 'It will be a big adjustment for Billie if she's not used to school.'

'Me too,' I sighed.

I honestly didn't know how Billie would react in a classroom situation. Because of her size, she wasn't a child who was hyperactive or would be running around. But I didn't know whether she'd be able to concentrate or have the discipline to sit still throughout her lessons.

After Louisa had gone, I went upstairs to check on the girls. As I pushed open their bedroom door, I saw that, not for the first time, Billie had climbed into Bo's bed and the pair of them were cuddled up in the bottom bunk.

It was obviously what they were used to doing at home but I always preferred it if children slept in their own beds so they didn't disturb each other. As gently as I could, I picked Billie up and put her back in the single bed over the other side of the room where she slept. It was a sign of how much weight she'd lost since arriving with me, as I'd never have been able to lift her when she first arrived.

In the morning, I got ready to take Billie to look round the school. She seemed curious but I don't think she fully understood yet what going to school meant.

'Will I get the jumper with the badge on it today?' she asked me excitedly.

'Yes, we can buy it at the school office when we're there,' I told her.

My friend Vicky had kindly offered to come round and sit with Bo for an hour while we were gone. She'd been a foster carer for years, like me, and at the minute she was fostering two boys who were both at school during the day. The previous week, I'd arranged for Vicky to meet us at the park so the girls had a chance to meet her before she looked after Bo.

The school was only a ten-minute walk away from my house and I knew the head teacher – a Scottish lady in her fifties called Mrs Moody. Several of my foster children had gone to the school over the years, although it had been a while since we'd last seen each other. Liz had already called her and given her some background about Billie.

When we arrived, she was already waiting for us in reception.

'Hello, Billie,' she smiled.

Billie looked very unsure and didn't say a word.

'Shall we have a little walk around and I'll give you a tour of the building?' she asked her.

'Don't like walking,' replied Billie.

'Come on, sweetie,' I encouraged her. 'You're a big girl, remember, and you can do lots of walking.'

Mrs Moody was a slight woman who moved quickly, and Billie huffed and puffed as she struggled to keep up with her. She seemed in awe of the school, though, and she looked on in wonderment as Mrs Moody pointed out the playground and the library.

'And this is where you'll have lunch,' she told her, as we walked into the school hall.

'Do you get Doritos and Snickers?' Billie asked her.

'The food is lovely here but I'm afraid we don't tend to have crisps or chocolate,' Mrs Moody replied.

'I think Billie will probably bring a packed lunch,' I told her.

It would be easier for me to keep an eye on what she was eating that way.

As we walked down the corridor, Mrs Moody pointed out the toilets.

'I do wees and poos in the toilet now and not on the floor like I did at Mummy's house,' Billie told her proudly.

'Well, that's very good, isn't it?' Mrs Moody replied, looking slightly taken aback.

'I've told Billie that if she's worried about accidents we can maybe arrange with her teacher to have a special cupboard in her classroom where she can keep a spare uniform,' I explained.

'Of course,' she smiled. 'I'm sure we can sort that out. And talking of teachers, this is Miss Senior,' she added.

A woman in her twenties walked towards us. She had long braids in her hair and a big smile on her face.

'Gosh, she looks really friendly and kind, doesn't she?' I whispered to Billie.

'Billie, Miss Senior is going to be your year three teacher,' Mrs Moody told her. 'I'm going to have a quick chat with Maggie now, so do you want to go and have a look at your new classroom?'

Billie looked at me and I nodded encouragingly.

'I'll be right here,' I reassured her. 'It's just for five minutes.'

Billie reluctantly followed Miss Senior, and I followed Mrs Moody into her office for a chat.

'To be honest, I don't know how Billie's going to settle,' I told her. 'She's had no formal education that we know of so she'll have to start from the very beginning.'

'I think we'll keep her in year three for now with children her own age and see how she gets on,' she nodded. 'We'll give her one-to-one support to help her with her reading and writing.'

'Behaviour-wise, I'm hoping she'll be fine,' I told her. 'Because of her size, she's not really a child who can't sit still or runs around. To be honest, my ongoing struggle is trying to get her to move more.'

'Well, there'll be lots of opportunity for running around at playtimes and during PE, and we'll encourage her to get outside and be active as much as possible,' Mrs Moody reassured me.

When Billie came back, she looked a bit overwhelmed.

'Did you like your new classroom?' I asked her and she nodded.

'Can I get the jumper with the badge on now?' she asked.

'Oh yes, you can buy uniform at the school office on your way out,' Mrs Moody told us.

She dropped us off there.

'Can I get three polo shirts and a couple of jumpers?' I asked the woman behind the office hatch.

She looked Billie up and down and frowned.

'The biggest size we have is age eleven to twelve,' she told me.

I knew instantly there was no way that was going to fit her.

'What is it, Maggie?' asked Billie. 'Is there no jumper for me?'

'They haven't got any left at the minute,' I told her. 'But you know what, we'll buy some school badges and then we can buy plain red jumpers and tops from somewhere else and sew your badges on.'

She nodded.

I hadn't weighed the girls but I was sure they'd been losing weight as they were eating healthier, more regular meals. They were both looking much slimmer by now, but even so, they were still significantly overweight for their age. Because Bo was under five, she was still under the care of a health visitor who was due to come round and monitor her weight.

We'd only just got back to the house and said goodbye to Vicky, when my mobile rang. It was Jenny. She was back from Scotland.

'It all went really well,' she told me. 'I met Tina's husband Don and her kids. They've got a lovely house, Maggie, I think Natalie's going to be really happy there. All the police and DBS checks have come back OK too.'

'That's really good news,' I said. 'Have you got any idea about timings?'

'Well, I'll have to check this with Tina, but if nothing else comes up, then there's no reason why Natalie can't go back to Scotland with her permanently after the funeral next week.'

'Wow,' I gasped. 'That's so soon.'

After I'd hung up, I went into the kitchen and put the kettle on. As I sat down at the table with a steaming cup of tea, I finally had time to think. It felt like there was so much going on at the minute.

I was so happy for Nat that she was going to get a fresh start after all that she'd been through, and I was confident that going to live with her aunt would work out. But, at the same time, I was also worried. She was still grieving for Peggy and I knew it was a lot of change for her to cope with all in one go. In the run-up to the funeral, Tina was coming back down from Scotland to clear out Peggy's house and then there was the funeral itself looming the following week.

I was glad that Billie wasn't starting school until the week after the funeral. It meant I could be there for Natalie and then concentrate properly on settling Billie in. I hadn't told the girls about Peggy's death because they'd never met her and also I felt that they were too young to understand. All they knew was that Natalie was a bit sad as they'd seen her crying a few times.

The next few days passed in a blur of arrangements. Tina came back down and Natalie spent the weekend at Peggy's house with her, sorting through her nan's things. The day before the funeral, Tina took her shopping for something to wear.

When Natalie got back, she proudly showed me the red dress that she'd chosen.

'Auntie Tina said people wear black at funerals but Nan didn't like black,' she told me. 'She liked bright colours and red was her favourite.'

'You're going to look beautiful,' I told her. 'Your nan would be so proud of you.'

Without warning, Natalie suddenly burst into tears.

'Oh, flower, what is it?' I asked, putting my arms around her and guiding her to a kitchen chair.

'I don't want to go tomorrow,' she wept. 'Can't I just go to school?'

'I know it's so hard for you, sweetie,' I soothed. 'But a funeral is an important way to celebrate someone's life and say goodbye to them.'

'B-b-but I don't want to say goodbye to Nan,' she sobbed. 'I want her to be back alive again.'

'Oh, lovey, I'm so sorry,' I told her. 'I'd give anything for Peggy to still be here too. But she's not and that's really, really sad but I think it's important for you to be there tomorrow.'

My heart broke for her but I'm a firm believer in children going to funerals when it's appropriate, as it can help them to process death and give them some sort of closure. Years down the line, I was worried that she would regret it if she didn't go.

'We'll all be there to support you,' I told her. 'Tina will be there and I'll be right beside you.'

'OK,' she sniffed.

Despite my reassurances, Natalie was understandably dreading the following day and I knew she'd had a restless sleep as I'd heard her getting up and down in the night. In the morning when she came downstairs, she looked exhausted.

'Try and have some breakfast,' I urged her gently but she only managed a few mouthfuls of cereal.

'I can't, I feel sick,' she sighed, pushing the bowl away.

Tina was coming to pick her up as they were leaving in the funeral car from Peggy's house.

'It's going to be OK,' I told her as she left. 'I'll see you there.'

As Louisa wanted to come to Peggy's funeral to support Natalie, I'd asked Vicky to look after Billie and Bo.

'I'm just going to pop out with Natalie for a bit because there's something we need to do together,' I told them.

I picked Louisa up on my way, as I was giving her a lift to the crematorium.

'I hate funerals,' she sighed, stroking her bump.

I suddenly realised that the last funeral that she'd been to was Dominic's. Only she and Charlie had been there and I couldn't even begin to imagine what it must be like to have to bury your own baby.

'You don't have to come if you don't feel up to it, lovey,' I told her, squeezing her hand. 'I don't want you to get too upset.'

'No, I want to be there for Natalie,' she told me firmly. I was so proud of what a kind, caring woman Louisa was, and I was grateful to have her with me.

It wasn't a big funeral. Peggy didn't have a large family so it was just Tina and her husband Don, who was a very tall, friendly man, as well as Natalie and a few friends and neighbours. As we walked into the chapel, I saw Natalie sitting at the front. She looked terrified and ashen-faced.

'Maggie, please can you sit next to me?' she whispered.

'Of course I will,' I told her.

I sat down on one side of her with Louisa next to me, and Tina sat next to her on the other side. As the organ started playing, we all stood up. Natalie grabbed my hand and I gave it a reassuring squeeze.

'It's OK,' I soothed. 'I'm here.'

As the undertakers carried Peggy's coffin in, I could feel Nat's whole body shaking. Even though I believed it was important for her to be here, it was lot for an eleven-year-old to cope with and it was devastating to see Natalie so upset. She sobbed throughout the service and all I could do was hand her tissues and put my arm around her. I couldn't stop my own tears from flowing either. I cried for Peggy and the awful disease that had taken her life and for Natalie and all that she'd lost.

It was almost a relief as we sang the last hymn – 'All Things Bright and Beautiful'.

'This was Nan's favourite,' smiled Natalie through her tears. 'I used to sing it at assemblies at my primary school.'

As we walked outside into the sunny spring day, Natalie and Tina gave each other a hug. Natalie had no more tears left now and seemed calmer, though she was obviously exhausted.

'That was a lovely service, Nat,' I told her. 'Peggy would be so proud of you.'

Poor Louisa looked distraught too – her eyes were all red and puffy.

'I'm a mess,' she sighed, once it was just the two of us again. 'Poor Nat. I feel so sorry for her. She's been so brave.'

Afterwards, we all went back to Peggy's house for a cup of tea and a few sandwiches but we didn't stay long.

'Maggie, can we go home now?' Natalie asked.

'Are you sure, flower?' I replied. 'You can stay here with Tina for as long as you want to and come home later.'

'No, I'm tired. I want to go back now,' she told me.

She looked utterly exhausted and I knew it was the best thing to do. She gave Tina big hug before she left.

'Thanks for coming, Maggie,' Tina told me.

'I wanted to,' I told her. 'I'm so sorry about Peggy.'

Tina explained that she was going to spend the next few days clearing the last few things from Peggy's house.

'I spoke to Jenny yesterday and, all being well, I should be able to take Nat back to Scotland with me,' she told me.

'That's great news,' I smiled.

It also meant we had a lot of sorting out to do, though. Natalie was going back to school for her last few days and I wanted to give her a little send-off.

'I'm not going to do anything too big but I want her to know we're all going to miss her,' I told Jenny when we spoke on the phone the next day.

We agreed that Jenny would pop in along with my supervising social worker, Becky. My friends Vicky and Carol were going to come as well as Louisa and Charlie and a couple of Natalie's close friends from school.

'Natalie's going to go and live with her Auntie Tina in

Scotland,' I told Billie and Bo that afternoon. 'So we're going to have a little party to say bye bye to her.'

'Are we going to live in Scotland too?' asked Billie, looking confused.

I shook my head.

'You're going to stay with me while Mummy and Liz do lots of talking,' I told her, and she seemed reassured.

Billie and Bo were excited about the party. I was going to do a buffet but I was worried about the girls gorging themselves on it. Louisa had promised that she'd keep an eye on them and she helpfully guarded the table after I'd filled a plate for each of them. I'd made Natalie a cake and put a candle on it, so she could blow it out and wish for happiness.

Halfway through the party, I realised Natalie was nowhere to be seen. I went upstairs to find her curled up on her bed, sobbing.

'Are you OK, flower?' I asked.

'Scotland's a long way away, isn't it?' she said tearfully. 'Maybe I should just stay here with you and Billie and Bo?'

I knew it was normal for kids to have a last-minute wobble.

'I know it feels like a long way away, Nat, but you're going to be with your family,' I told her. 'I can see how much Tina loves you and I know how much your cousins are looking forward to having you live with them.'

'But you're my family too,' she said, her lip trembling.

'And we'll always be here for you,' I reassured her. 'You're welcome to come and stay here whenever you want to. In fact, Tina was telling me how she likes to go to Devon every year on holiday so I said you must call in on the long journey. That way, I can see you and I can meet your cousins. How about that?'

She nodded bravely.

'But I'll miss Louisa's baby being born,' she sighed.

'We will ring you and text you as soon as he or she arrives and send you lots of pictures, I promise,' I told her.

'But being here reminds me of Nan and I can pretend she's just down the road,' she whispered. 'I might forget her if I go to Scotland.'

'You'll never ever forget your nan, flower,' I told her. 'You and Tina will talk about her all the time and I know you've got some of your Nan's things and photos from her house. Speaking of which, I've got a little goodbye present for you.'

I went to my bedroom and came back with a small black box.

'Tina was telling me about Peggy's favourite earrings,' I said.

'Oh, those shiny white round ones?' smiled Natalie.

'Yes, the pearls,' I nodded. 'Well, as you haven't got your ears pierced, I got Peggy's earrings made into something special for you.'

She opened the box.

'A necklace!' she gasped.

'You can wear it every day and think of Peggy,' I told her. She smiled.

'Now don't be sad, lovey, or you'll set me off,' I joked. 'Come on, let's go down and finish the party.'

I knew that had been our special goodbye.

The next morning was hectic as Tina arrived to drive Natalie back to Scotland. The car was already pretty full with some of Peggy's stuff so it took us a while to squeeze Natalie's things in there as well.

When the time came for them to leave, I could see tears forming in Natalie's eyes. I tried to keep everything casual and upbeat as I didn't want her to be upset when she left.

'Give me a ring when you arrive, just to let me know you've got there safely' I told her. 'And I'll speak to you soon.'

As I gave her a final hug, I hoped she couldn't see the tears in my own eyes.

'You take care, flower, and we'll see you very soon,' I told her and she nodded bravely. 'You can call me whenever you like, and I'll always be here for you, Nat.'

Billie, Bo and I stood at the front window and waved them off. As I watched the car disappear out of sight down the street, my heart felt heavy with sadness that another child had gone.

EIGHT

Clues

It always felt a bit strange after a child had left. Even though I was still busy with Billie and Bo, Natalie's absence was very noticeable to me. It was the little things that over the past year or so had become habit. I found myself wandering into her room to sort through her washing basket, only to find it empty. It looked so cold and bare in there without her piles of books and the odd socks and pyjamas scattered across the floor that always used to annoy me. One morning, I heard the post thud onto the mat and I realised it was the children's newspaper that Natalie liked to read each week and I'd forgotten to cancel the subscription.

She sent me lots of texts, although they were usually very short, and sometimes I had to get Louisa to help me decipher some of the abbreviations that she used. But I spoke to Tina on the phone and thankfully things seemed to be going well. It was early days, but Natalie liked her new school and Tina and Don were decorating her bedroom for her.

With Nat gone, it freed me up to devote all of my attention to Billie and Bo. A few days after Natalie left, we had their Looked After Child (LAC) review. This was a meeting that normally happened in the first few weeks of a placement arriving and it was chaired by an Independent Reviewing Officer, or an IRO, as we called them for short. This was usually an experienced social worker who worked for Social Services but someone who wasn't involved directly in the case and could represent the children's best interests.

The LAC review was being held at Social Services, where I was introduced to the girls' IRO – a woman called Michelle. She was in her thirties, smartly dressed with a very business-like manner.

'I recognise your face, Maggie,' she told me as she gave my hand a vigorous shake.

'I don't think we've worked together before but you've probably seen me around at Social Services,' I smiled. 'I come to a lot of meetings here.'

She'd already met the girls, as well as Mandy, as she'd popped into one of their contact sessions to say hello.

As well as Michelle and I, there was Liz, my supervising social worker Becky and Janet the contact worker who had been running the sessions with Mandy. Normally, someone from the child's school would be invited to attend but as Billie hadn't started yet, we didn't think it was worth Mrs Moody taking the time out to come along. Mandy had been invited too but no one seemed sure whether she was going to turn up or not.

'Let's get started and then if she does come, we can fill her in,' said Michelle.

Liz outlined why the girls had initially been taken into care nearly a month ago. She talked about the concerns about the neglect and their weight. She pointed out that Billie hadn't attended mainstream school and neither of them were toilet trained.

'We believe Mandy has some learning difficulties,' said Liz. 'We don't know yet to what extent but we're starting a parenting assessment to see whether she can learn to parent adequately if she's given the skills and knowledge.'

'What role does Jim, Mandy's brother, have in all of this?' asked Michelle.

'He's part of the extended family in that he lives in the same house,' explained Liz. 'He's a long-distance lorry driver so his work takes him away around three or four nights a week.

'He'll be subject to police and Social Services checks but in terms of parenting, the assessment will be looking purely at Mum's ability to parent on her own.

'I believe Jim has a contact session coming up so it will be interesting to see how the girls respond to him,' she added.

That led us to talk about contact.

'How are the sessions with Mum going?' Michelle asked Janet.

'Mandy is very likeable,' she smiled. 'She's got an innocent, childlike quality about her, but watching her with the girls it sometimes feels like there are three kids in the room.'

'In what way?' asked Michelle.

'Well, she doesn't mind rolling around on the floor with the girls and seems as excited to play with the dolls as they are.

'I've never seen her set any boundaries for the girls or pick them up on their behaviour and the girls seem to be the ones in charge rather than her.'

We also talked about the endless battle with her bringing food to contact.

'Most sessions, she'll turn up with two big carrier bags full of sweets, chocolate and crisps and if we don't step in, the girls will just gorge themselves on them,' sighed Janet.

'I know Liz has had a word with Mandy and I've asked her a few times, but even though we've expressed our concerns about the girl's weight, she still hasn't quite grasped why it's not a good idea.'

When it was my turn to address the meeting, I talked about my ongoing battle at home to wean them off junk food and onto regular meals as well as encouraging them to have fresh air and exercise.

'I've got a note here to say the health visitor's going to be coming round every few weeks to monitor their weight and they're on vitamin D supplements for rickets?' asked Michelle.

'Yes, that's right,' I nodded.

'Billie starts school next week so I think that will be good for her. And what about Bo?'

'I'm going to start toilet training her and eventually look at getting her into some sort of childcare setting – either a nursery or a playgroup for a few hours a day. She's very much dominated by Billie so it's going to be interesting to see how she is on her own,' I added. 'She didn't say much at all when she first came to me but her speech is already developing.'

Michelle took down lots of notes.

'Is there anything else you want to mention, Maggie?' she asked.

'There's been a few bits of odd behaviour but I'm recording everything for Liz and Becky and it's nothing that I can't handle.'

'OK,' smiled Michelle. 'It's still early days so I think we carry on as we are and see where we're at in another six weeks or so.

'For now, the plan is for the girls to remain with Maggie and start school and nursery. I think that, alongside her assessment, it would be a good idea for Mandy to start some parenting classes during the day, particularly anything that looks at nutrition and cooking, and then eventually we can see if the girls can stay at the contact session for tea with Mandy in charge.'

A couple of days later, Billie faced one of her biggest challenges – starting school. She was really looking forward to wearing a uniform so I'd done as I'd promised and bought some plain red jumpers and polo tops from ASDA in larger sizes and sewn the school badges on myself. We'd also chosen a matching red headband with a bow on it and some hair slides with the money Mandy had given the girls.

'At your next contact session, Mummy will be able to see you in your school uniform,' I told her. 'And you'll be able to show her the lovely hair slides that she bought you.'

For once, Billie didn't say much and I could tell that she was nervous.

'Where's Billie going?' asked Bo, looking confused as we left the house.

'I'm going to school, Bo Bo, cos I'm a big girl,' Billie told her proudly.

Both girls still found walking difficult and moved slowly, so I'd allowed us plenty of time to get there. As we approached the school gates, Billie gripped my hand tightly.

'Oh, look,' I pointed. 'Miss Senior's there waiting for you.'

She waved at us as we headed towards the classroom.

'You're going to have such a great day,' I told her. 'You've got your packed lunch and your new pencil case. I can't wait to hear all about it.'

Billie still looked very unsure and as Miss Senior led her into the classroom she kept turning back to look at us. Finally, she turned and gave me a sad wave, and I could see the fear in her eyes.

'See you soon,' I called, smiling broadly to reassure her.

In a way, Billie going to school was a good distraction for me as today was also the day when Louisa and Charlie were going for their twenty-week scan. I felt sick with nerves for them. I'd tried to call Louisa last night but Charlie had picked up and said she wasn't feeling great and had gone to bed.

'I know she must be so anxious about tomorrow,' I'd said. 'Tell her I'll be thinking about her and if she feels up to it to give me a call after your appointment tomorrow. I hope everything goes OK,' I'd added.

'Me too,' he'd sighed.

I felt so sorry for Charlie. He'd taken Dominic's death badly and I knew he'd found it hard to know how to support Louisa as well as dealing with his own grief.

I'd planned a quiet day at home for me and Bo as I wanted to get her started on toilet training. I was dreading it but, unlike Billie, she seemed to quickly get the hang of it. I think it helped that she'd seen Billie go through it before her, so she knew what to do. In between trips to the loo, I constantly checked my phone both for calls from school and messages from Louisa. I'd told Mrs Moody that I thought it would be best for Billie to do full days right from the start as she'd missed so much schooling, but I prayed that she was OK.

Bo seemed to be enjoying the time on her own without Billie interfering and controlling what they did. She particularly loved the Barbies and the huge plastic house I'd picked up years ago from a charity shop. I tidied up the kitchen and out of the corner of my eye, I watched her play. She got the Barbies and took all of their clothes off. Then she put them in the bed, one on top of the other, facing each other.

'What are those dollies doing?' I asked her.

'They're sisters,' she grinned. 'Like me and Billie.'

'There are two beds in that bedroom,' I told her. 'So each sister can have their own bed.'

'But Billie's my sister and she sleeps in my bed,' said Bo matter-of-factly.

'I know,' I said. 'And I move her back again.'

Bo carried on playing with the dolls. I was sorting through some washing when suddenly there was a knock at the door. I went to open it and was shocked when I found Louisa standing on the doorstep.

'I wasn't expecting to see you today, flower,' I gasped. 'How did it go at the hospital?'

She burst into tears and my heart sank. She must have seen the distraught look on my face as she thrust something into my hand. There was no mistaking the grainy black-and-white scan picture.

'Meet your granddaughter,' she smiled through her tears.

'Oh my goodness,' I gasped, my own eyes filling with tears. 'And she's OK?'

'She's absolutely perfect,' grinned Louisa. 'I'm so relieved, I don't think I've stopped crying since.'

'Oh, lovey,' I sighed, wrapping my arms around her and giving her a hug. 'I'm so happy for you and Charlie.'

'Obviously there are no guarantees but all the measurements were fine and everything else looks good,' she told me.

I wanted to burst with happiness.

'A little girl,' I sighed. 'I'll have to start knitting.'

'If you don't mind, Maggie, I still don't feel ready to do all that again,' she sighed. 'We might get a few things out of your loft eventually but I still can't bring myself to get excited.'

'I understand, lovey,' I told her.

I knew she wouldn't allow herself to relax until she was holding her little girl in her arms, but for now, everything was going well. As Bo and I walked to school to pick up Billie, it felt like a weight had been lifted.

'How did she get on?' I asked Miss Senior as I collected her from the classroom.

'Good, I think,' she told me. 'She's been very quiet and slightly bemused by it all but her learning-support assistant guided her through everything and explained what we were doing.

'She also took her to the toilet regularly.'

'That's great,' I replied.

Billie looked tired and was slower than ever as we walked home.

'I'm hungry,' she sighed.

'You can have a snack as soon as we get home, sweetie,' I told her. 'How was school?'

'OK,' she replied. 'There were lots of other kids there and we sat at tables and looked at words. It went on a very long time, Maggie.'

'You'll soon get used to it,' I smiled.

As far as I was concerned, today was a good day. I had a healthy granddaughter on the way and Billie had spent her first ever day at school without any major incidents or meltdowns.

Over the next few days, I enjoyed my time at home with Bo.

The toilet training had been going well until one morning she refused point blank to go.

'Bo, the timer's gone off so we need to go and try and do a wee,' I told her.

She shook her head.

'We can't have you doing a wee on the floor,' I told her. 'And remember, you want to be a big girl like Billie, don't you?'

After a lot of persuading, she reluctantly followed me to the toilet. But as she sat there, she started to cry.

'Ouch,' she sobbed, her bottom lip wobbling. 'It hurts.'

'What hurts, flower?' I asked and she pointed between her legs.

'It hurts when you do a wee?' I questioned, concerned, and she nodded.

As I always did when a new child arrived, I'd already registered the girls with my GP, so I made an appointment for the following day.

'We're going to go and see the doctor today,' I told Bo.

She looked terrified, but the GP was lovely, kind woman in her fifties who had a really gentle manner. After a lot of persuasion, I got Bo to go for a wee into a pot and the doctor quickly examined her.

'We'll send the sample off to the lab, but it sounds like she's got a bit of an urinary infection,' she told me. 'I also noticed that she's a little bit sore and inflamed down below.'

'Oh,' I replied, surprised. 'What can cause that?'

'With young children like Bo it could be that they're touching themselves a lot down there,' she said. 'Is that something you've seen her do?'

'Not really,' I shrugged. 'Her elder sister does that, but I've never seen Bo do it.'

'Perhaps it's something she does at night?' suggested the GP. 'It can be a bit of a comfort thing. Anyway, it's worth keeping an eye on it, and I'll give her some antibiotics to help with the infection.'

I mentioned it to Liz and made a note in my recordings that Bo had seen the doctor, and what the outcome had been.

Over the next few days, Bo seemed a lot better as the antibiotics kicked in. Billie had been at school exactly a week when my mobile rang one afternoon. My heart sank when I saw the number that flashed up on the screen.

It was Billie's school.

'I wanted to have a quick word with you, Ms Hartley, as it's difficult to talk at pick-up time and Billie will be there,' Miss Senior told me.

'Please call me Maggie,' I replied. 'What's happened?'

'Billie is absolutely fine,' she reassured me. 'There was an incident in class this morning that I just thought I should mention to you.'

I listened as she described how the children had finished their writing work and were sitting on the carpet listening to a story before lunchtime.

'One of our teaching assistants noticed that Billie was . . .' Her voice trailed off and she paused.

'Er, how can I put this?' she sighed. 'She noticed that Billie was masturbating.'

'Oh no,' I gasped.

'The TA took her out and explained that it wasn't appropriate behaviour in the classroom.'

'Billie's very immature for her age and we're still working on what's acceptable,' I explained.

'Of course, I completely understand,' Miss Senior replied. 'I know it's a difficult time for her being taken into care. It was just a bit of a surprise.

'I was thinking perhaps if she wore a pair of tights that might help discourage it from happening again?'

'I understand,' I told her. 'But because of Billie's size I would honestly struggle to find a pair of tights to fit her. Anything that would fit her around the waist would be way too long in the leg.'

I also had the same issues with trousers.

'I could try and get her a pair of shorts with an elasticated waist?' I suggested. 'But I'll also talk to Billie about it at home tonight.'

I didn't want to tell Billie off or make her feel shameful about exploring her body, but she needed to know when and where it was appropriate to do it.

That night, we had a little chat before bedtime when Bo was brushing her teeth.

'Billie, Miss Senior said you were touching yourself at school today when it was story time,' I gently told her. 'Remember we don't touch our noo noos when other people are around.'

I would normally use the correct terms when I talked about bodies, but I wanted to say it in a language Billie understood, so I used the terms that she used.

'Oh, I was only tickling,' she told me, looking confused.

'Well, we don't tickle ourselves down there with other people around.'

It was odd behaviour for a seven-year-old. In fact, there were so many things recently that had really started to niggle at me. I had to remind myself that Billie had been through so much change and upheaval recently and now she'd started school as well. Touching herself was possibly a comfort thing, as the doctor had said. Once she got used to school, hopefully she would settle down a bit.

NINE

Bombshell

Bo looked at me quizzically.

'It's OK, sweetie,' I reassured her. 'Step onto the scales.'

'But why?' she asked.

'This is what Nancy wants you to do,' I nodded. 'She needs to make sure that I'm looking after you properly.'

Nancy was the health visitor who, every month, was going to come round and monitor the girls' weight. I was always careful not to talk about weight loss or diets around them. They didn't know they were obese and I didn't want them to feel any stigma due to their weight as it wasn't their fault. Young children are reliant on adults to make healthy choices for them.

As soon as Nancy had weighed them both, they went off to play in the living room.

'Well, everything's going in the right direction,' she told me, writing it down. 'They're losing weight steadily, which is great.'

I hadn't put them on a diet as such. They were just eating regular meals, having healthier snacks and I was encouraging them to move around and walk more. They still had a long way to go until they were in the normal boundaries for their age, but it was reassuring to know that things were moving in the right direction.

I'd also been taking them to hospital every few weeks for blood tests.

'Their vitamin D levels look a lot better now and their calcium is up too,' smiled Nancy as she read their notes.

'Yes, they're doing really well,' I nodded. 'They'll need to have X-rays as they get older to check the rickets hasn't had any lasting effects on their bones, but they're moving round a lot easier these days.'

I didn't know whether it was the weight loss or if their bones and joints were less painful, but I'd noticed they weren't hobbling as much, which was a relief to see.

I didn't know whether it was because the health visitor had been or whether Billie was still adjusting to school but the girls seemed particularly tired that night, so I put them to bed early.

They'd been in bed for half an hour when I decided to send a text to Natalie to see how she was.

'Damn,' I sighed to myself when I realised my phone was in my bedroom. Wearily, I trudged up the stairs and, as I passed the girls' room, I was sure that I heard someone crying. I quickly backtracked and put my ear to their door. It was definitely someone sobbing.

Then a voice yelled: 'No, Billie. No!'

I pushed open the door to find Billie curled up in Bo's bed. They both blinked as their eyes adjusted to the brightness of the landing light. I could see that Bo's face was wet with tears.

'Bo, what is it, sweetie?' I asked her gently. 'You two should be fast asleep by now. It's very late.'

'Billie's tickling me,' she sobbed. 'Me want to go to sleep.'

She seemed quite upset.

'Billie, I need you to get back to your own bed now, please,' I told her firmly, walking across the room with her.

'Now, I don't want to see you getting out of your bed again,' I told her. 'Your sister's really tired and you've upset her.'

'I was only playing,' sighed Billie.

'It's bedtime, not playtime,' I replied.

I went over to Bo and stroked her hair until she stopped crying.

'It's OK,' I soothed. 'Billie's not going to bother you now.'

She was exhausted and I could see her eyes closing. Before I left the room, I went back over to Billie.

'I'm going to leave this door open so I'll hear you if you get out of your bed again, OK?'

Billie nodded.

'Night night,' I told her.

Every evening, I put them to bed separately but still, more often than not, Billie would always crawl into Bo's bed. I knew I needed to keep an eye on it and be more vigilant about getting her to stay in her own bed.

A few days later, the girls had a contact session with Mum. This time it was different as their Uncle Jim had been invited to come along as well. I know both Liz and I were curious to see how he interacted with the girls.

I still wasn't sure what the girls thought of their uncle. They didn't talk about him very often so I was keen to see how both the girls and Mandy were around him.

'You're going to see your Uncle Jim today,' I told them as we pulled up outside the contact centre.

'And Mummy?' asked Bo.

'Yes, Mummy will be there too,' I reassured her.

Jim and Mandy were already there.

'Hello, girls,' he said as we walked into the contact room.

They were both very quiet and hid shyly behind my legs. Mandy was quiet too and the atmosphere in the room was very stilted. It seemed as though no one knew quite what to say.

'Billie, why don't you show Mummy the book you got from school?' I suggested.

I'd picked up Billie straight from school so she was still in her uniform and had her bag with her. She walked over to Mandy and sat on her lap.

'I can do reading,' she told her proudly.

Jim burst out laughing.

'There ain't no use showing your mum a book,' he scoffed. 'She can't read a bloody thing. Can't write neither. She's stupid,' he told me and Liz. 'Thick as two short planks, that one.'

'Mummy can look at the pictures,' Billie told him firmly, scowling at him.

'You watch your lip, young lady,' he told her. 'Don't be giving me cheek.'

Mandy didn't seem bothered by Jim's words, and she just giggled.

'Girls, why don't you find those baby dolls that you like?' suggested Liz.

'Oh I love playing baby dolls,' smiled Mandy, getting off the chair and lowering herself onto the floor.

'What are you doing, Mand?' hissed Jim. 'Get up off the floor and come and talk to the adults. Leave the toys to the girls.'

She did exactly what he asked, and looked down at the floor as she came to sit beside him.

'She's like a big kid sometimes,' he sneered. 'And big's the right word when it comes to her.'

By the end of the session, I could see that Jim was very much in charge. He was aggressive in his manner and when he said jump, everyone around him jumped. Mandy seemed to want Jim's approval and the girls tiptoed around him.

At the end of the session, I stayed with the girls while Liz showed Mandy and Jim out.

'Do you fancy a quick cup of tea?' she asked me when she came back in.

'Girls, you can play for a bit longer while Liz and I make a drink in the kitchen,' I told them.

We left all the doors open so we could still see them. Luckily, there was no on else in the contact centre so it was fine for them to play there.

'That was a bit strange,' sighed Liz. 'What did you make of Jim?'

I shrugged.

'He was very controlling and domineering,' I told her. 'And he certainly likes putting Mum down.'

'Yes, that wasn't very nice to hear, especially in front of the girls,' sighed Liz. 'I was almost tempted to say something to him.'

Jim didn't seem the most pleasant man but, from what I'd seen, he wasn't threatening in any way and the girls didn't seem scared of him.

'When he's in the room, he's the one who's in charge,' nodded Liz.

Neither of us were sure yet where Jim fitted into this puzzle of a family but I was sure there was still lots to find out.

That night, when we got back from the contact centre, I could tell both girls were shattered. Billie was still getting used to school and Bo always seemed worn out after contact. After dinner, I ran a warm bath to help relax them and they had a good soak.

'Come on then,' I told them after twenty minutes. 'It's time for bed now.'

'Let's get you out, little one,' I said to Bo.

I put the little step next to the bath like I always did. Bo heaved herself up then climbed carefully down onto the bath mat.

'Let's get you dry, flower,' I told her, wrapping her in a towel.

Billie was old enough to get herself dry so I wrapped her in a towel and got her to dry herself and put on her pyjamas.

After I'd finished drying Bo, I handed her her pyjamas.

'You try and put then on yourself like a big girl,' I told her, keen to encourage her independence.

While she did that, I picked up their dirty clothes from the bathroom floor. I'd just walked out onto the landing to put them in the washing basket when I heard a yelp.

I spun round and dashed back into the bathroom. Billie was standing next to Bo, who had her pyjama top on but not her bottoms. Suddenly Bo burst into tears.

'No,' she sobbed, pushing Billie away. 'Don't wanna do tickling today.'

'But you like the tickling game, Bo Bo,' Billie told her in a baby voice.

'No,' yelled Bo. 'Don't like it.'

I rushed over to them.

'What's going on, girls?' I asked them. 'Why's Bo crying?'

'I was just playing a game with Bo Bo but she was being mean,' huffed Billie.

'What sort of a game?' I asked. 'It's not a good game if it's making your sister upset.'

'It's a tickling game,' she told me.

Before I could register what was going on, Billie walked towards Bo.

'Tickle tickle, Bo Bo,' she laughed as she rammed her hand between Bo's legs.

Bo let out a cry of pain and pushed her away.

'Ouch,' she whimpered. 'It hurt my noo noo, Maggie.'

I quickly ran over to them and pulled Billie away. I crouched down on the floor so our eyes were on the same level.

'Billie, that is Bo's body and she is telling you that she doesn't want you to touch her, OK?' I told her firmly.

'That isn't a game. You don't touch other people's bodies, just like nobody touches your body.'

'Yes, you can,' laughed Billie. 'We do it all the time at our house.

'Bo Bo likes having her noo noo tickled, don't you, Bo Bo?'

Bo was getting really upset now.

'No,' she huffed. 'Don't like it.'

'She's lying,' spat Billie.

What I was hearing was suddenly making me feel really uncomfortable.

'Why don't you go and wait in your bedroom and I'll be there in a minute, lovey?' I told Billie. 'I'm just going to take care of Bo.'

As I helped Bo into her pyjama bottoms, she was still quietly sobbing.

'I'm sorry Billie hurt you,' I soothed. 'I won't let her do that to you again.

'She shouldn't be touching your noo noo like that.'

Bo snivelled and shook her head.

When she was dressed, she followed me into the bedroom where Billie was sitting on the bed, looking cross.

I was careful to keep my voice very casual and light as I started to ask questions.

'I don't know about the tickling game,' I told her. 'So why don't you tell me what you do to Bo when you play it?'

'Come on, Bo, let's show Maggie what we do,' Billie said excitedly.

'No, no,' I replied firmly. 'Why don't you try and tell me with your words.'

'Well, Bo lies down and goes like this . . .'

Billie lay on the floor on her back and opened her legs.

'. . . then we play the tickling game or sometimes the pokey pokey game.'

My heart thumped out of my chest and I felt sick. I needed to know exactly what had been going on.

'What's the pokey pokey game?' I asked, dread rising in my stomach.

'I go like this,' said Billie, showing me her pointed finger. 'And I go pokey pokey in Bo's noo noo.

'Or you can do it with toys and dolls and stuff. You just push them in.

'And sometimes if Bo's a really good girl then I kiss her noo noo.'

I'd done my best to hide my emotions and stay calm but Billie must have seen a flicker of horror on my face.

'It's OK, Maggie,' she smiled. 'Bo likes it. And then when she's a big girl she can do it to me because that's what sisters do.'

'Where's Mummy when you're playing this game?' I asked her.

Billie shrugged.

'Downstairs with Uncle Jim cos we do it at night time.'

'Have you played this game for a while?' I asked her.

'Oh yeah,' Billie told me proudly. 'For a very, very long time.'

It was bedtime and I needed to remain calm for the girls but inside my whole body was recoiling in horror. I'd discovered a secret that was about to change everything and I felt sick to my stomach.

TEN

Emergency Measures

Absolute panic filled my chest. What the hell was I going to do? It was 7.30 at night, both girls were in their pyjamas and I could see they were exhausted, but I knew there was no way on earth I could put them to bed in the same room.

Think, Maggie, think, I willed myself.

I took them both downstairs to the living room and I put the TV on to buy myself a bit of time. Bo climbed onto the sofa and Billie plonked herself next to her.

'Billie, will you sit in this chair, please,' I asked her, pointing to the armchair. 'I want to give Bo a cuddle because she's a bit upset.'

I couldn't risk them being anywhere near each other at this stage.

'Are you OK, flower?' I asked Bo.

She'd stopped crying now and she seemed a little bit calmer. I sat there next to her in a daze, so many questions racing through my head.

How long had this been going on? How had I not known? Why had I not spotted the signs?

Bo let out a big yawn and I knew I had to get my act together and get the girls to bed.

'Billie, please will you come upstairs with me for a minute?' I asked her.

'But I'm watching telly,' she sighed.

'Come on,' I told her firmly. 'I need your help with something.'

Bo was thankfully engrossed in the cartoons that were on and seemed OK for now.

'I've just had a really good idea,' I told Billie as we walked up the stairs. 'You're such a big girl now, going to school and everything, so you should have a bit of a later bedtime than Bo. So what I thought we'd do is move you to your very own big girl's bedroom so you didn't wake up Bo when you came to bed.'

Billie looked confused.

'Which is the big girl's bedroom?' she asked me.

'The lovely room near my bedroom,' I smiled.

'Natalie's one?' she asked.

'Well, now that Natalie doesn't live here any more, it's going to be your room,' I told her. 'So you and I are going to move some of your things so you can sleep in there tonight.'

'But I like my old bedroom with Bo Bo,' she sighed.

'Oh, this new bedroom is going to be perfect for you,' I told her, being as persuasive as I could. 'It's got a desk in there so we can buy you a special pot to put your pencils and pens in so you can sit at your desk and do some writing or drawing.'

Billie didn't look convinced, but I knew there was no other option. I quickly stripped her bed and made up the single bed in Natalie's old room with Billie's bedding on it so it felt familiar. I put the little lamp on so it looked more homely and got Billie to carry in the teddy from her bed and a few of her books and toys.

'I know the Barbies are your favourite so you can bring a couple of those too if you want,' I told her.

As she picked them up, I was suddenly reminded of that time in the kitchen a few days ago when Bo had put the dolls on top of each other in the same bed and said they were sisters.

She'd been telling me then what had been going on and I hadn't picked up on it.

Then there was the urinary infection and the bruising the doctor had noticed down below. It hadn't been from Bo touching herself, it had been caused by her own sister.

There was no point dwelling on it. Now I knew what had been happening, I had to focus on what happened next.

Once it had some more of Billie's bits and pieces in it, Natalie's old bedroom looked a lot more cosy. There was one final thing I needed to do before I put the girls to bed. I went into the cupboard on the landing and pulled out a stairgate. I screwed it across the doorway of Bo's bedroom so that way I knew that Billie wouldn't be able to go in there. Looking back, it had always been her getting into Bo's bed and not the other way round. Then I got a set of little bells attached to a string that I tied to the top of the gate. It was something I always did with the stairgate because I knew that children, especially older ones, could learn how to undo them quite easily, so if I heard the bells ringing, it would alert me to the fact that someone was tinkering with it.

Billie watched me do all this with a puzzled look on her face.

'Why is Bo having that on her door?' she asked curiously.

'It's to make sure that if she gets up in the night then she can't go wandering out in the dark,' I told her. 'We don't want her to fall down the stairs or hurt herself, do we?'

Billie shook her head.

'And remember, flower, this is Bo's room and you've got your new big-girl room,' I told her firmly. 'And you don't go into each other's bedrooms unless I'm with you, OK?'

Billie nodded.

We went back downstairs where thankfully Bo was still glued to the TV.

'Billie, you can watch a bit of telly now while I take Bo up to bed,' I told her.

I took Bo upstairs and showed her Billie's new room.

'This is Billie's big-girl bedroom,' I told her. 'She's going to sleep in here from now on so that she doesn't disturb you.'

Bo looked around, her eyes wide with confusion.

'Where me sleep?' she asked.

'You've got your lovely big bedroom all to yourself,' I told her as we walked down the landing.

'What dat?' she asked as she saw the stairgate over the doorway.

'That's your own special gate with jingly bells on,' I smiled. 'So if you get up in the night and you need me you can ring your bells and I'll come straight away, OK?'

Bo nodded, although she looked a bit bemused by it all.

'And in the morning I'll come and wake you up and if you get up before I do then you can shout for me. I've put some toys in your room from downstairs so you can have a play.

Bo let out another huge yawn and I could see that she was exhausted.

'Let's get you into bed,' I told her gently.

I tucked her in and stroked her long, dark hair.

'You sleep well, flower,' I soothed. 'I've told Billie that she's not allowed to come into your bedroom without me being there, OK?'

She nodded.

'Me not like the tickling game, Maggie,' she mumbled as I turned off the light.

'I know you don't, sweetie,' I sighed. 'Neither do I and I'm going to make sure that Billie's not going to play it any more.'

I went downstairs and sat with Billie for ten minutes to give Bo time to settle, then I took her upstairs to her new bedroom. Now wasn't the time for any more questions or serious discussion. All that could wait until the morning.

'Isn't it lovely and cosy in here?' I smiled.

Billie shrugged.

'Remember to stay in your own bedroom and Bo will stay in hers,' I told her firmly. 'I'll come and wake you up in the morning and if you wake up first it's fine to go to the toilet but it's not fine to go anywhere else, OK?'

She nodded wearily.

There was no way I was going to go downstairs. I wouldn't be able to relax until I knew both girls were asleep, so I sat in my bedroom with the door open so I could hear exactly what was going on. I wanted to make sure that they stayed in their own bedrooms and that Billie didn't try and get in with Bo.

I also knew I needed to let Liz and Becky know exactly what had gone on, so I got out my laptop and typed a long email to both of them. I explained exactly what had happened, what Billie had disclosed and the precautions that I'd taken.

Twenty minutes later, I crept out of my bedroom and went to check on them. I gave a sigh of relief when I found them fast asleep, both in their own bedrooms.

Now I knew the girls were settled, I went downstairs and phoned my fostering agency. I spoke to the duty social worker – a woman called Emily

'Something happened tonight that I need to ring in urgently,' I told her.

'Oh, Maggie,' she sighed after I told her the whole story. 'What a shock.'

'I know,' I told her. 'It's completely floored me.'

Emily was going to call Social Services and let them know what had gone on.

'I'll let you know what they say,' she told me.

They were the ones who would decide what would happen next and I knew there was a real chance they might decide it was too much of a risk to keep the girls in the same house tonight. I hoped that wouldn't be what was decided, as the idea of waking one of the girls up and having to move them to another carer was just too much to bear.

Emily called back half an hour later.

'I've just got off the phone to the local authority and they're happy with the measures that you've put in place for tonight,' she told me. 'They've alerted the girls' social worker and she'll be in contact with you first thing in the morning.'

I knew there would be an urgent meeting to decide what happened next. In all honesty, I didn't know what to do from here.

I couldn't sleep at all that night. I constantly had one ear out, listening for the creaking of a floorboard or the tinkling of a bell. I was so paranoid that the girls weren't in their own rooms, I checked on them every few hours. Thankfully, they were both fast asleep but I couldn't rest.

I was sitting at the kitchen table with a cup of tea as it got light outside. As the sun came up over the garden, I gave a big sigh. I was dreading today and what it was going to bring. What had happened last night still didn't seem real and I hadn't fully had a chance to process it yet. I knew I would feel better when I'd talked things through with Liz and Becky.

I was still lost in my thoughts when I heard Bo shouting for me from upstairs. I rushed up to her room, worried I was going to find Billie in there, but she was standing there alone at her stairgate.

'Are you OK, sweetie?' I asked her and she nodded.

Billie was still fast asleep so I went and woke her up.

'How was your first night in your new bedroom?' I asked her.

'OK,' she said.

Everything seemed entirely normal as we went through the usual morning routine of getting Billie ready for school. The only thing that was different was that I couldn't leave the girls on their own with each other. I made sure that they both used the bathroom separately and got dressed in their own bedrooms while I watched them like a hawk.

As we were walking Billie to school, my phone pinged with a text from Liz.

I got your email and have called Becky. We'll come round to your house for an emergency meeting at 9.30 am.. Hope that's OK?

I quickly typed out a reply.

That's fine. See you both then.

When we dropped Billie off, I didn't mention anything to Miss Senior about what had happened. Again, that would be something that we needed to discuss at the meeting.

As soon as we got back from the drop-off, I got Bo settled with a drink and some toys in the kitchen.

'Liz and a lady called Becky will be here in a minute,' I told her. 'We need to have a chat so when they come, we're all going to go into the living room.

'You can keep playing but if you need anything give me a shout, OK?'

Bo nodded but she was happily engrossed in her game with the Barbies.

Becky arrived first.

'How are you, Maggie?' she asked.

'OK,' I sighed. 'Still a little shellshocked, to be honest.'

'I'm not surprised,' she replied sympathetically.

Liz arrived shortly afterwards. I made us all a cup of tea and we sat down in the living room.

'I couldn't believe it when I read your email, Maggie,' said Liz.

I went through with them exactly what had happened and what I'd done, moving them into separate bedrooms.

'You did exactly the right thing, Maggie,' nodded Liz.

'But what do we do now?' I asked. 'I've never dealt with sexual abuse between siblings before.'

'Is it definitely abuse, though?' asked Liz. 'Or is it just normal exploration?

'A lot of younger children are curious about their bodies and I suppose their sibling is the closest person to them if they want to explore.'

That hadn't been something that I'd even considered.

'I feel that it is abuse,' I sighed. 'Last night, Bo was upset and she definitely didn't want Billie to touch her, but Billie wouldn't listen. She got quite insistent and forceful, and Bo didn't have the strength to make her stop.'

Billie was older, she was the one with the power and, to me, there had been an element of force or coercion used.

'Liz, Bo was saying no and she definitely didn't want this to happen,' I told her.

I explained how a lot of other things were making sense now, like the infection Bo had and the bruising the doctor had found.

'Billie has hurt her,' I said. 'To me, that's abuse.'

'Do you think putting them in separate bedrooms and keeping an eye on things will be enough?' asked Becky.

I hesitated.

'I don't know,' I sighed.

'Do you think it was a one-off?' asked Liz.

I shook my head.

'This is clearly something that's been happening for a long time. Billie said they'd done it all the time at their mum's house. The sad thing is that I think Bo has tolerated it for a long time.'

I didn't have any of the answers either, just a lot of questions. Was it safe to keep the girls together? Although they were only four and seven and not teenagers, I couldn't help but wonder if that mattered? Abuse was abuse, wasn't it? If it was an older boy and a younger girl I wasn't sure we'd be having the same conversation. It seemed likely that one of them would be moved automatically. I just didn't know what to think.

'My view is, let's wait and see what happens,' said Liz. 'We know what's been going on and the girls are in separate bedrooms now.

'You've told Billie that it's not acceptable so it might not happen again.'

'Maggie, do you think it's manageable?' asked Becky.

'I can try,' I nodded.

'The thing that worries me the most is finding out where this behaviour come from,' I added 'Is this really normal exploration? In my opinion this isn't something a seven-year-old thinks of doing themselves.'

Liz shrugged.

'But we know that Billie is immature for her age. Perhaps this is a normal curiosity about bodies? It's a bit like when young children play doctors and nurses.'

I wasn't convinced that the things Billie had talked about doing to Bo were things that young children would even think about.

'I can't help but feel that there's more to this than meets the eye,' I told them.

To me, it raised all sorts of uncomfortable questions. Was Billie picking up on something that she'd seen at home? Often in chaotic households, children witnessed all sorts of adult sexual behaviour or were exposed to pornography. Did Mandy have a boyfriend that we didn't know about?

'I think you're right, Maggie,' nodded Liz. 'It's definitely something we need to look into more and talk to Mandy about.'

For now, though, our main and most immediate priority was to make sure Bo was protected and safe in this house.

'OK, let's keep an eye on it for the next couple of days,' said Liz. 'Maggie will keep the girls apart as much as possible and let's see what happens.'

So that's what I did. It was fine during the day when Billie was at school, but as soon as she came home, I had to have my eye on the girls all of the time and I couldn't leave them on their own together. I stopped giving them a bath together and they each got dressed and undressed in their own bedrooms.

It was stressful. Before I did anything, I had to do a quick risk assessment in my head. If I put the washing in the machine, I had to have one or the other child with me. If they were both playing in the garden, I had to be out there with them. If they were both watching TV in the living room, I couldn't be in the kitchen making dinner. Even going to the loo was impossible as I couldn't leave them alone together even for a few minutes.

One night, after I'd put the girls to bed separately, I went downstairs. I'd already sat in my bedroom for half an hour to make sure that both the girls had settled and neither of them were out of their beds.

I was in the kitchen emptying the dishwasher when I heard an almighty crash from upstairs. It was followed by a high-pitched scream that made my blood run cold.

I bolted up the stairs, as quick as my middle-aged body could carry me. I found Billie lying on the landing floor on top of the stairgate from Bo's bedroom door. It had completely come off the doorway. Bo was stood in her bedroom, crying hysterically.

'No, Billie,' she sobbed. 'You can't come into my bedroom.'

She looked terrified of her big sister, and my heart sank. It was in that moment that I knew it was impossible. I couldn't keep Bo safe any more.

ELEVEN

Separation

Some days, things just don't go to plan and today was one of them. I always tried to be organised on a morning so everyone was dressed and ready and we could get Billie to school on time. I even allowed extra time for the fact that the girls still got quite out of breath and walked very slowly.

But today, everything had gone wrong. My head was still reeling from what had happened with the stairgate the night before. I'd struggled to sleep again and this morning I'd dropped Bo's entire bowl of cornflakes on the kitchen floor. By the time I'd cleaned up the mess and taken the girls upstairs to get dressed, we were already behind schedule. I left Billie to get dressed in her room while I helped Bo in her bedroom so I could make sure that the girls were kept apart.

When I went back to check on Billie, however, she was still in her pyjamas and playing with her Barbies.

'Billie, we're going to be so late,' I told her firmly. 'Hurry up and brush your teeth, sweetie.'

Twenty minutes later, both girls were finally ready.

'Shoes on now,' I told them in the hall. 'Come on, as quick as you can.'

We were just about to go out the front door when I realised my handbag with my keys inside was upstairs in my bedroom. It would literally take me seconds to run up and get it. Both girls were waiting by the front door with their shoes and coats on and if I took one of them with me, it would take for ever.

'Wait there, I'll be back in a jiffy,' I told them.

I bolted upstairs and scanned the room for my handbag. A few seconds later, I found it on the bed underneath my dressing gown.

'Right, girls, let's go,' I yelled, but as I came down the stairs, my heart sank.

Billie had pinned Bo up against the hallway wall. She'd pulled up her skirt and was about to force her hand down her sister's pants.

'Tickle, tickle, tickle,' she laughed.

I thundered down the stairs as fast as I could.

'Billie, what on earth are you doing?' I yelled.

Bo looked terrified and as I pulled Billie away, she burst into tears.

'Billie, you have got to stop that,' I told her. 'Remember what I said last night? We don't play that game in this house any more. You're hurting Bo and she doesn't like it.'

Billie looked shellshocked as I gave Bo a cuddle.

'Are you OK?' I asked her and she nodded.

I went over to Billie.

'You really need to listen to your sister, Billie,' I told her. 'This is her body, it's private and she doesn't want you to touch her like that, OK?'

Billie looked sullen.

'But I wanted to play the tickling game,' she said, stamping her feet angrily.

'Well, it's not happening here any more Billie,' I told her.

It worried me deeply that Billie was getting more aggressive and more brazen. I'd already told her this game wasn't appropriate and that Bo didn't like it, but she still continued to do it and she didn't seem to care who saw it.

'Come on, let's get you to school,' I told her.

We were so late that, instead of walking like we usually did, I drove us to school. On the way there, I tried to lighten the mood and completely change the subject.

'You've got PE today, Billie, that will be fun, won't it?' I told her. 'And Bo when we get home perhaps you might like to go out and play in the garden?'

'Me put wellies on?' she asked excitedly.

'Yes, you can put your wellies on,' I told her. My heart broke at how young and innocent she still was, and all that she had had to endure at the hands of her own sister.

As soon as we'd dropped Billie off, I knew I needed to get back and call Becky. I'd already emailed her and Liz about the stairgate incident last night and I needed to update them about what had happened this morning.

'Are you OK?' I asked Bo on the way home. 'Did Billie make you feel sad this morning?'

'Me not like the tickling game,' she muttered.

'I know you don't, sweetie,' I told her. 'It's not a very kind game.'

She was very quiet on the rest of the drive home, but she soon cheered up when I helped her get her wellies on and she wandered out into the garden. While Bo was occupied playing, I picked up my mobile and called Becky. I couldn't ignore what my gut was telling me any longer.

'This isn't working, Becky,' I sighed. 'I can't keep them both safe. It's just not manageable.'

'I got your email about what happened last night,' she replied. 'It does sound as though it's getting a little bit out of hand.'

I told her about the most recent incident this morning.

'Billie's getting more aggressive and I can see Bo is becoming increasingly scared of her,' I told her. 'What's even more worrying is that Billie's willing to do this quite openly in front of an adult with absolutely no shame about it. This isn't a game or two young kids being curious about their bodies, Becky, it's sexual abuse.'

'I think you're right, Maggie,' she sighed. 'My feeling is that Social Services need to separate the girls as soon as they can and find out from Billie exactly where this game has come from.'

I also told her how I was struggling to manage it.

'It's fine in the day when Billie's at school but the rest of the time it's really tricky,' I continued. 'I'm watching them like a hawk and I can't relax. I can't even go to the loo and leave them.

'I'm terrified that if I take my eye off them for one minute then Billie will try and hurt her sister, which is exactly what happened this morning. I was barely gone for thirty seconds.'

'I'll talk to Liz and get her to call you,' Becky promised.

Liz rang me back straight away.

'Becky told me what happened this morning and I've seen your notes about last night,' she sighed. 'What's your feeling about things, Maggie?'

'I know we always try our hardest to keep siblings together but my gut is telling me that I think we need to separate the girls,' I told her. 'My opinion is that it's no longer safe to keep them together.'

No matter what I thought, though, I knew ultimately it was Liz and Social Service's decision.

'I agree with you, Maggie,' she replied, and my heart sank with relief. 'We can't afford to take any risks, particularly when it comes to sexual abuse, and it's becoming clear that this is what we're dealing with here. I think we need to move Billie as a matter of priority.'

It was a tough decision, but I was glad to hear that she felt the same.

'But where will she go?' I asked. 'Who on earth is going to want to take her?'

I knew it wasn't going to be easy to find her a new foster carer.

Any potential carer would have to be told what had gone on at my house. Because of safeguarding issues, Billie couldn't go to a home where there were younger children living there. Even if she went to another carer with older children, would they really want to take on a child who had been suspected of sexually abusing her own sister?

'There are some carers who only take on single placements,' Liz told me. 'So someone like that who didn't have any other children in the house would be ideal.'

But I knew there weren't many of those around, especially someone with an immediate vacancy. I also knew that if they couldn't find a suitable carer today then Billie would have to go to a children's home. The idea of that broke my heart.

'I'll start ringing round now and let you know,' Liz told me.

'When do you think it will happen?' I asked.

'For Bo's safety, I think we need to move Billie ASAP,' said Liz. 'Ideally today, if possible. I'll let you know.'

As I put down the phone, I felt sick. Although my gut was telling me that this was the right thing to do, I knew how upsetting and confusing it was going to be for both girls. They'd only been with me for six weeks and they'd already had so much change in their young lives. Despite everything that had happened, I knew that Bo loved her big sister, and I was worried about the impact it was going to have on her to see her sister sent away.

Bo and I spent a quiet morning at home. To be honest, my head was all over the place. All I could think about was Billie and who on earth was going to agree to take her. Even though it had been a collective decision, the burden of responsibility weighed very heavy on my shoulders.

What if we were splitting them up for no reason? What if I was being overcautious and this was just a phase?

But I'd seen the fear in Bo's eyes last night and Billie's blatant disregard for how Bo might feel or the fact that it was wrong given that she'd felt it was OK to do it when I was around.

Any joy? I texted Liz.

No luck as yet I'm afraid, she replied.

As I watched Bo play in the garden, giggling and chattering away to herself, I couldn't help but think how much easier it would be to find a home for her. Everyone would want the victim and not the abuser.

And, just like that, the solution came to me.

I phoned Becky again.

'What if I keep Billie and Bo is the one who moves?' I suggested. 'I'm sure Liz could easily find someone to take her.'

'That's true, Maggie,' replied Becky. 'But it would also mean that while Billie was with you, you wouldn't be able to foster any other children.'

'I'm prepared to do that,' I told her.

It would break my heart to say goodbye to Bo so soon, and I didn't want her to think she was being punished for what had happened, but deep down, I knew it was the best solution for both the girls. It would also give me the chance to do some work with Billie and try and get to the root of where this behaviour had come from.

'If you're sure, then I'll ring Liz now and suggest it,' Becky told me.

'I'm positive,' I replied firmly.

Now, all I could do was wait. It was just after lunch when Liz called back.

'Thanks so much, Maggie,' she told me. 'You were right. I managed to find a foster carer to take Bo pretty quickly.'

It was a woman called Angela who lived around half an hour from me. She had two biological sons who were seven and nine and her and her husband, Dan, were also fostering a thirteen-year-old girl. I'd heard my friend Vicky talk about Angela but I'd never met her.

'I've arranged for you and Bo to call into her house for a cup of tea after you pick Billie up from school,' Liz told me. 'I think it would be good for Billie to come along too.'

'So I shouldn't mention anything to the girls about why we're going there?' I asked.

'No,' said Liz. 'I think it's best that they meet Angela and visit the house and then I'll come round and talk to them after you get back.

'Also, Angela wants to meet Bo first before she definitely commits.'

This way, at least the girls would know who Angela was, and Bo wouldn't feel like she wasn't going to live with a complete stranger. She wouldn't have spent a lot of time with her but she'd have seen her house. I knew it was important for Billie to know where her sister was going to be living, too.

Bo and I went to pick Billie up from school and when we'd all got back in the car, I twisted round in my seat to talk to them.

'I thought we'd go and see a lady called Angela today,' I told them, keeping my voice light. 'She's a foster carer too, so she looks after children, like me. We're just going to pop round to her house for a cup of tea.'

I held my breath as I waited for their reaction. Thankfully they both seemed to accept it and neither of them asked any questions. I knew it was important not to say anything at this stage, as Angela might decide after meeting Bo that she didn't want to take her on after all.

Angela's house was a 1930s semi-detached house on a quiet cul-de-sac.

'Look, there's a doggy at the window!' yelled Billie excitedly as we pulled up outside, and neither of them could wait to get out of the car.

'Me see the doggy too,' chirped Bo.

I'd never been so grateful to see a dog in my life.

A woman who I assumed was Angela answered the door. She was in her early thirties with blonde hair tied back in a ponytail. She looked like she'd been running as she had gym leggings and a T-shirt on. The girls squealed with delight as the golden retriever ran around their legs.

'Hello, Maggie, I'm Angela,' she smiled. 'And this is Ziggy,' she said, pointing to the dog.

'This is Billie and Bo,' I told her.

'Come on in,' she told us.

The girls followed the dog straight through the house and into the garden where two blond-haired boys were playing.

'Those are my two sons, Max and Milo,' she told me. 'Katie who we're fostering is at an after-school club and I'm afraid my husband Dan's still at work.'

She made me a cup of tea and we chatted. She was very easy to get along with and I knew Bo would instantly warm to her.

'So, tell me about Bo,' she said. 'Liz explained a little bit but it's always good to know the full picture from the foster carer.'

I told her about the struggle with the girls' weight, the rickets, how we were still trying to assess the relationship between the girls and their mum.

'They're having regular contact twice a week,' I told her.

I also explained about what had happened with the tickling game, what Billie had told me and what had happened since then.

'Gosh, that's awful for both of them,' sighed Angela. 'Where on earth has a game like that come from?'

'That's what we need to get to the bottom of, to be honest,' I told her. 'We didn't know at first whether it was normal exploration, just a one-off or something more sinister, but understandably, Social Services don't want to take any chances.

'We need to know that Bo is safe while we talk to Billie and try and find out more.'

'Absolutely,' she nodded.

I knew it would be good for Angela to spend a bit of time with the girls so I called them in from the garden.

'I thought you girls might fancy a game of Dobble,' she told them. 'Have you ever played that before?'

Bo shook her head shyly. Angela showed the girls how to play it and she had a very gentle, patient nature.

I didn't want us to overstay our welcome, so after an hour I told the girls we had to go.

'It's been nice to meet you,' Angela told them. 'Hopefully I'll see you again soon.'

'Thanks for letting us come round,' I told her.

'I'll give Liz a ring now,' she smiled.

On the drive home, the girls were full of chatter about the dog.

'Angela's really nice, isn't she?' I smiled.

'Me like Ziggy,' grinned Bo.

'Yeah, I liked the doggy too,' nodded Billie.

We'd only been back fifteen minutes when Liz texted.

Just spoken to Angela. She's happy to go ahead.

I arranged for her to come round and talk to the girls in an hour after I'd had chance to give them some tea. I'd already made spaghetti bolognese so I all I had to do was heat it up. I was still clearing away the dishes when Liz arrived.

'How did it go?' she asked me quietly.

'Good,' I nodded. 'She's got a dog, which was a big hit with both of the girls, and she seems like a really nice woman.'

But no matter how lovely Angela was, I was still dreading what was about to come. The girls were watching telly in the living room.

'Bo, sweetie, will you come into the kitchen a minute?' I asked her.

Billie was so engrossed in the cartoon, she didn't even register Bo leaving the room.

'Maggie tells me you went to see a nice lady called Angela today,' Liz smiled.

'She had a big doggy,' Bo told her. 'It licked my face.'

'Oh yuck,' laughed Liz.

'No, me like it,' smiled Bo. 'The doggy was funny.'

'He was called Ziggy, wasn't he?' I told her and Bo nodded.

Liz took a deep breath and I felt my stomach clench.

'Maggie's been telling me about the tickling game and how it makes you feel a bit sad.'

'Me not like it,' nodded Bo.

'Well, what Maggie and I were thinking was you can go and stay with Angela for a little while. Then we can talk to Billie about the tickling game to see if we can make it stop.'

'Will the doggy be at Angela's?' she asked.

'Yes, Ziggy will be there,' I told her.

'Can I take my Barbies?' she asked.

'Yes, you can take a couple of them,' I reassured her.

'Is Billie coming too?'

'No, Billie won't be coming to Angela's,' Liz told her. 'She's going to stay here with Maggie.

'But you'll still see her when you see Mummy at the contact centre and you'll still see Maggie when she drops Billie off.'

I'd been prepared for tears or tantrums, but Bo totally accepted it all. At the end of the day, I had to remember that she was only four. She didn't really understand what it meant and she was more interested in the dog than anything else.

'Why don't you go and watch telly and Maggie and I will have a talk to Billie now?'

I waked back with her to the living room, where Billie was still watching TV.

'Guess what, Billie?' beamed Bo. 'Me going to live with Ziggy at Angela's house.'

Billie's face fell.

'Come on, flower, come and have a chat with me and Liz,' I told her gently.

We went into the kitchen.

'Why's Bo going to live with Ziggy?' she asked, her eyes filling with angry tears. 'Am I going to live with Ziggy too?'

Liz and I exchanged looks.

'Bo's going to live at Angela's house for a little while,' Liz explained. 'Nobody's done anything wrong, we just need to keep everybody safe and we've decided that this is the way we're going to do it.

'You're going to stay here at Maggie's and you'll still see Bo at contact with Mummy.'

Billie's face fell and I could see that she was close to tears. In amongst all this, it was important to remember that she was still a little girl herself, who didn't understand that what she was doing was wrong.

'When is she going?' Billie asked.

I looked at Liz.

'She's going tonight,' Liz told her. 'Maggie will start getting her things together now.'

'But why can't Bo Bo stay here?' she asked, her bottom lip trembling.

'It's not the right thing at the minute, flower,' I told her. 'We need to keep you and Bo safe, so we think it's best for you two not to live in the same house for a little while.'

Billie blinked back the tears and I put my arm around her.

'It's going to be OK,' I soothed. 'I'll be here and you'll still be able to see Bo.'

'But I don't want her to go,' she sighed.

She burst into tears and curled up in my arms. Whatever had happened, my heart went out to her and all my instincts were telling me that she was as much a victim in all of this as Bo.

TWELVE

Goodbyes and Questions

There is no easy or good way to separate siblings. It was always difficult and one of the worst parts of being a foster carer. In the past, it was something that had been so hard for me to accept, but, in this case, all of my instincts were telling me that there was no other way. Splitting the girls up was our only option to keep them both safe.

I sat with Billie and held her as she cried. All I could do was reassure her that everything was going to be OK and that she would still see Bo. Whatever had happened, she was just a vulnerable seven-year-old girl who'd been taken away from her home and her family. After all she'd been through, she felt like she was losing her sister now, too.

'You'll be OK,' I soothed. 'I'm here for you and you'll still see Bo. In fact, you'll see her at contact tomorrow.'

'Tomorrow?' she sniffed.

'Yes, you've got your contact session with Mummy after school.'

That seemed to cheer her up a little bit and she wriggled

herself free from my arms. Liz handed her a tissue and she patted her eyes dry.

While Billie stayed with Liz, I went into the living room to see Bo.

'I'm going to go upstairs now and pack your things to take to Angela's with you,' I told her. 'Do you want to come and help me?'

She nodded eagerly.

'I get my Barbies,' she replied.

I knew there was no way I could pack everything tonight. Some of Bo's clothes were in the wash and she had things scattered all over the house. Over the next few days I'd gather them all together and bring them to contact for her.

While Bo sorted through her toys, I chatted to her again about why she was moving to Angela's. I didn't want her to feel like she was being punished or sent away.

'Nobody's done anything wrong, you know, Bo,' I told her, as I folded up her clothes and put them into a suitcase. 'We just need to talk to Billie about the tickling game as we know you don't like it and we need to help Billie understand that. And while we're doing all of that talking, we know that you'll be safe and well looked after at Angela's house.'

'With Ziggy?' she added.

'Yes with Ziggy,' I smiled.

The dog was proving to be a bit of a godsend in all of this.

'Come on, flower, let's go and say goodbye to your sister,' I told her after I'd packed as much of her stuff as I could.

As we walked downstairs, Billie and Liz were coming out of the kitchen. Billie's face fell as she saw the suitcase I was holding.

'Oh, is Bo Bo going now?' she gasped.

'I'm afraid so, lovey,' I told her.

'I need to get Bo to Angela's house so she can get settled before bedtime,' Liz explained.

'And remember, you two will see each other at the contact centre tomorrow,' I reminded them.

I handed the suitcase to Liz and she took it to her car. Bo happily followed her down the front path while Billie hung back, a pained expression on her face.

'It's going to be OK,' I told her, giving her hand a quick squeeze. 'Let's go and say goodbye to your sister.'

We're doing the right thing, I repeated to myself. *There are no other options.*

Besides, it might not be for ever. If things were able to be resolved then there was the possibility that both girls could live together again in the future.

Liz opened the passenger door of the car for Bo. But just before she got in, she stopped and turned around.

'Bye, Billie,' she said, giving her a little wave.

'Bye, Bo Bo,' Billie replied sadly. 'See you tomorrow.'

But Bo had already got into the car and slammed the door.

'Come on then, flower,' I said gently. 'Let's go back inside.'

Billie didn't run but she shuffled as fast as she could down the front path, into the hallway and the living room. She pressed her face against the glass of the front window and watched mournfully as Liz's car disappeared off down the road.

'Come on, let's run you a bubble bath,' I told her. 'I bet a nice fluffy bath will cheer you up.'

But Billie didn't answer. The tears that she couldn't hold back any longer spilled down her face. I gave her another hug.

'I know it's been a really hard day for you,' I soothed. 'And you and Bo have been so brave.'

I ran Billie a bath, hoping that it would help in some small way. She carefully lowered herself in off the step and she closed her eyes as she sank into the warm water.

'Maggie, did Bo go away because of me?' she asked suddenly. 'Have I been bad?'

'It's nobody's fault, and no one has been bad,' I told her. 'Bo didn't like the tickling game, and you, me and Liz need to do lots of talking about that. In the meantime, we need to make sure both you and Bo are safe so that's why she's gone to Angela's house.'

I didn't want her to feel any guilt or shame.

While Billie dried herself and got into her pyjamas, I went downstairs to make her a warm milk. While I was in the kitchen, my mobile rang.

It was Angela.

'How's it going?' I asked her. 'How's Bo doing?'

'She's fine,' she told me. 'I think she's missing Billie and she wondered if she could say goodnight to her?'

'Of course,' I replied.

By then, Billie had wandered downstairs so I put the phone on speaker and handed it to her.

'Is that you, Billie?' asked Bo down the phone.

'Hi, Bo,' she said nervously.

'We went for a walk with Ziggy,' Bo told her. 'I throwed him the ball and he catched it.

'I'm going to bed now. Night, Billie.'

'Night night, Bo Bo,' she said sadly and passed the phone back to me.

My heart broke for these two confused little girls, and I could see the realisation dawning on Billie that it was bedtime and Bo was somewhere else.

'That was nice of Bo to ring,' I told her as I put my mobile down on the worktop, but Billie looked annoyed.

'She's been on walk with Ziggy,' she told me. 'That's not fair. Why can't we have a dog?'

'Dogs are a lot of work,' I told her. 'And I'm not sure I've got the time to look after one.'

I could see that Billie was exhausted and I knew what I needed to do now was get her to bed. I was relieved that she'd already had a couple of nights in her new bedroom, so at least she'd started to get used to sleeping without Bo.

I was worried that she'd be unsettled after such a traumatic day so I kept conversation to a minimum and sat on her bed and read her a story to help her relax. As I turned the pages, I could see her eyes were already heavy.

'Night night, flower,' I told her, closing the book. 'It's been a long day so try and get some rest.'

'Night,' she mumbled sleepily as she turned over onto her side. I left the bedroom door slight ajar and the landing light on to reassure her if she woke up.

It had been an eventful and sad day and as I walked back downstairs, I felt shattered too. It felt strange without Bo in the house, like something was missing. It was the same feeling I'd had after Natalie had gone. Although I was devastated for Billie, for me there was also a sense of relief that Bo had gone. It meant that I didn't have to be on my guard constantly. I would be able to go to the loo or be in the kitchen and make dinner without always having to worry about where the girls were.

I opened up my laptop and wrote up my notes about what had happened and emailed them over.

Just as I'd pressed 'send', my phone beeped with a text from Becky.

How did it go today? Hope you are holding up.

It's done, I typed. *Billie's very sad but doing OK.*

Afterwards I made myself a cup of tea and I phoned Vicky for a chat. I didn't want to burden Louisa with my worries and as Vicky was a foster carer too, it meant I could chat in confidence to her and she understood what I was going through.

'I'm so sorry I haven't spoken to you for a while,' I told her before explaining what had gone on.

'You know me, Vicky, and you know how much splitting up siblings goes against all my beliefs,' I told her.

She knew that in the past I'd fought tooth and nail to keep sibling groups together.

'It sounds like you had no choice, Maggie,' she told me. 'You can't afford to take any chances with sexual abuse.'

'I know, but it doesn't make it any easier to cope with though,' I sighed. 'There's a seven-year-old girl upstairs whose heart is broken.'

I felt better for talking things through with someone.

'So what happens now?' Vicky asked.

'We just need to get to the bottom of where this so-called game has come from and what was going on at home.'

'It's not normal for a seven-year-old to come up with something like this off her own bat,' replied Vicky.

I agreed with her. At that young age, children weren't sexually mature or interested in sex. What worried me the most was that, if Billie hadn't made this game up herself, where had it come from? I was convinced there was more to this than meets the eye, we just needed to find out what.

Children thrive on routine and it helps make them feel secure.

I was keen to keep everything as normal as possible for Billie, so the next day, I took her to school as usual. I didn't say anything to Miss Senior as I knew that was Liz's responsibility.

Liz had already texted me to say that she'd called a professionals' meeting which was happening at Social Services later that morning. A professionals' meeting is often described as a meeting of minds. It tended to happen when Social Services weren't sure how to proceed in a case and they wanted input and advice from the police or other outside agencies. Billie's headteacher Mrs Moody was going along, as well as Liz, her manager and someone from the police and child protection. What frustrated me the most about these meetings was that foster carers were generally not invited to attend them. At the end of the day, foster carers know the child in question better than anyone and are with them every day. It always feels like a bit of a slap in the face that we're not seen as professionals and are not involved in the decision-making. It made me feel very frustrated and out of the loop.

It wasn't until Liz popped round later that I found out what had been discussed.

'How's Billie?' she asked.

'She's still very sad and I think she's missing Bo, although she seems to have channelled that into being annoyed about the dog,' I told her.

'Oh yes, I think the dog has really helped settle Bo,' she smiled. 'Angela said Bo had had a peaceful first night.'

'So what happens now, Liz?' I asked her. 'Where on earth do we go from here?'

Liz filled me in on what had happened at the professionals' meeting that morning.

'We talked about the tickling game and whether it was just playing and exploring, or was it something more sinister?' she said.

'And what was the conclusion?' I asked.

'I think everyone felt it could just have been children exploring, but once you'd been made aware of it, acknowledged it and explained that Bo didn't like it, it still continued. In fact, it feels like Billie actually became more aggressive and deliberately targeted Bo even in front of other adults.'

'What was the police's view?' I asked.

'They felt that we'd done the right thing in separating the girls and they do feel that it's worth investigating.'

It had been decided that Liz would talk to Billie, Bo and Mandy separately and try and find out what each of them knew about this game and where it might have come from.

'Depending on what comes out of that, the police will then have a chat with them and take a view from there,' she told me.

Liz explained that she'd already asked Mandy to come to the contact centre before her session with the girls that afternoon.

'I'm going to tell her that Billie and Bo have been separated and explain why and then ask her a few questions.'

'Good idea,' I replied. 'I'll see you then.'

I headed to the contact centre after I'd picked Billie up from school. Bo was already there when we walked in.

'Bo's been telling me all about the doggy in her lovely new house,' smiled Mandy, totally oblivious to how Billie might be feeling.

'I don't like dogs,' said Billie icily. 'They're stupid.'

Janet, the contact worker, tried to distract the girls with some toys, but Billie snatched a doll off Bo and there were a few little arguments. I could see Billie was taking her anger and frustration out on her sister.

Janet was supervising the session so Liz and I were able to pop out into the kitchen for a chat.

'How did it go with Mandy?' I asked her. 'How did she react to the fact that girls had been separated?'

'I'm not sure it really sunk in,' shrugged Liz. 'She didn't seem particularly upset about it or worried about how the girls were.

'She was more interested in what Angela's house was like.'

They'd also talked about the tickling game.

'I asked her if Bo had played it at home and where she might have got it from,' said Liz.

'And what did she say?' I asked.

'She went bright red and got all giggly. Then she said she didn't know anything about it and completely clammed up.'

I felt like we were banging our heads against a brick wall and were no nearer to the truth.

'I need to talk to Billie,' sighed Liz. 'I won't do it tonight as she'll be tired after contact but I'll come round tomorrow after school.'

'That's fine,' I said.

I was curious to see what Billie was going to say. I knew it was good to keep things informal as children were more likely to open up if they were relaxed and playing. Young children don't tend to respond very well if they're told an adult wants to talk to them or if they have to sit down at a table with them. It can make them worried and nervous that they've done something wrong.

When Liz arrived the next day, Billie was playing with some Barbies in the kitchen. I made Liz a cup of tea and she sat down on the floor next to her.

'Are you bringing Bo back today?' Billie asked her.

'No, I'm afraid not, Billie,' Liz replied. 'She's staying at Angela's house for now.

'Why do you think Bo has gone to Angela's house?' she asked her.

'Cos she didn't like the tickling game,' replied Billie, engrossed in playing with her dolls.

I busied myself in clearing away some dishes but I was still listening intently to the conversation.

'Why don't you think Bo liked the tickling game?' continued Liz

Billie shrugged.

'She used to like it. We played it all the time at our house and she never cried like she did at Maggie's.'

Liz paused.

'Billie, did you make the tickling game up or did somebody teach you how to play it?'

Billie didn't look up and carried on playing with the Barbies.

'Billie, did you hear what I asked you?' urged Liz. 'Did you make the tickling game up or did somebody teach you?

'It's really important that you tell us.'

I held my breath.

'Somebody teached me,' she replied.

'Was it a grown up who showed you how to play the tickling game?' asked Liz.

Billie nodded her head.

Liz and I looked at each other.

'Can you tell me who the grown up was?' asked Liz gently. 'It's really important that we know, Billie.'

I held my breath as I waited for her to answer.

'No,' she sighed suddenly. 'Don't want to do talking no more.'

And with that, she carried on playing with her dolls while Liz and I stared at each other in shock.

THIRTEEN

Peeling Potatoes

It was what I'd feared the most. At the back of my mind, I knew that children who sexually abuse others, especially a child as young as Billie, had potentially been sexually abused themselves. I'd always hoped that wasn't the case with Billie, but from what she'd just revealed to us, it seemed it was. It was a learned behaviour and she was very much a victim too.

Poor, poor girl.

Liz tried to ask Billie more questions but she wouldn't say anything else. I could see the more she pushed, the more Billie was clamming up and I didn't want her to feel like she'd said or done something wrong.

'Billie, would you like to watch some telly now?' I asked her and she nodded.

Thankfully, she didn't seem upset as I took her into the living room.

'You have a bit of a chill out and then it will be dinner time soon,' I smiled as I put on some cartoons.

I went back into the kitchen to talk to Liz. I think we were both in shock.

'It's horrendous,' I sighed. 'Who on earth would make a child play such a sick game?'

I knew there was no other family apart from Mandy and their Uncle Jim around as when the girls had first come into care, Social Services had checked there was no one else who would be able to take them on.

'Did the girls come into regular contact with many other adults?' I asked Liz.

'I don't know,' she shrugged. 'But that's what we need to find out.'

From the impression I'd got, the family had led quite a reclusive life. The girls hardly went out and we knew Billie had never gone to school.

'As far and I'm aware, the only adults in their life were their mum and Jim,' sighed Liz.

My head was spinning. Liz and I looked at each other and I knew what we were both thinking but neither of us dared say it.

'I need to talk to my manager,' she said firmly. 'But after what Billie's just told us, I think it's time to involve the police.'

Liz left to go back to the office and talk to her manager while I went and sat with Billie on the sofa. As I watched her, laughing away at the cartoon, I wanted to cry. It was just abhorrent to think that someone could do that to a seven-year-old girl. This so-called tickling game had obviously become part of life for Billie and up until now she didn't know it was wrong. For all we knew, it could just be the tip of the iceberg, and I dreaded to think what else she might have been subjected to.

Liz rang back as I was making dinner.

'I contacted the police and someone from CID is going to come round to the house tomorrow and speak to Billie,' she told me. 'It will be a plain-clothes female officer and I'll be there too to introduce her.'

Liz explained that the idea wasn't to interview Billie there and then. Because of her age, they thought it would be better for her to meet the police officer at home in a more relaxed setting. Then the following day she'd be interviewed at a specialist interview suite.

'Hopefully that way it won't be too intimidating or scary for her,' Liz explained.

'OK,' I said. 'And what about Mandy and Jim?'

'The police don't want to question them until they've spoken to Billie,' she told me.

'And what about the contact sessions?' I asked.

Often, contact with birth families was stopped while a police investigation was taking place.

'Well, the next session with Mandy isn't for another three days so we'll take a view once the police have spoken to Billie. Plus, all the sessions are supervised and I can be there too and make sure there's no talk about the investigation or the tickling game.'

It was going to be an intense few days ahead for Billie. While she was playing in her bedroom, I gave Becky a quick call to update her about what had happened. I told her what Billie had said.

'Oh, Maggie, that's awful,' she sighed. 'Poor Billie. Have you got any thoughts about who the grown up might be?'

I paused. In my mind, everything pointed to the same person.

'I didn't say anything to Liz because I didn't think it was my place but I'm sure she was thinking exactly what I was. They led such a sheltered life and the only man around the girls is Uncle Jim.'

'Does Billie talk about him a lot?' Becky asked.

'No, not really,' I sighed. 'Not much at all in fact.'

But I described how I'd seen him being aggressive and controlling with both Mandy and the girls at contact and how the girls had seemed keen to please him.

'Well, I'm sure he'll be questioned by the police as a priority,' said Becky.

I didn't try to ask Billie any more questions about the tickling game that night. In fact, I deliberately went out of my way not to mention it. As a foster carer, once the police were investigating an allegation you had to be incredibly careful that you were not asking the child any leading questions or that you could be accused of putting ideas into their head.

Thankfully, Billie seemed oblivious to the bombshell that she had just dropped. As I tucked her in that night, she didn't seem upset or distressed.

'You have a lovely sleep, flower,' I told her. 'And I'll see you in the morning.'

In a way, her calmness made it even more tragic. Abuse had become such a normal part of day-to-day life for her. I knew she was going to face a lot of questions over the next few days and my heart went out to her.

By the time we got back from school the next day, Liz was already parked outside the house waiting for us.

'I just thought I'd pop in and say hello,' she told Billie.

While I made Billie a drink and snack, Liz chatted to her.

'I was talking to a lady I know called Jemma today,' she said casually. 'You know all those questions we've been asking you about the tickling game?'

Billie nodded.

'Well Jemma's really clever and very kind and I think she'd be a great person to try and help us sort it out. In fact, she said she might pop in and say hello to us this afternoon. Would that be OK with you, Maggie?' she asked.

'Yes, of course,' I nodded. 'I like kind people and Jemma sounds very nice. Tell her to pop in for a cup of tea.'

'Is that OK with you, Billie?' Liz asked her.

I'm not sure she'd even been listening but she shrugged.

Liz didn't want to tell her at this stage that Jemma was from the police as we didn't want to worry her.

Jemma arrived half an hour later. I went to meet her at the door.

'DC Jemma Lyons,' she smiled, showing me her ID. 'You must be Maggie.'

She was in her thirties with long dark hair and Liz had been right – she had a kind, gentle manner that I knew would put Billie instantly at ease.

'Billie's with Liz in the kitchen,' I told her.

We all went through and Jemma introduced herself to Billie.

'What are you playing?' she asked her.

'Barbies,' she replied, looking away shyly.

'Oh, my little girl Rose loves her Barbies,' Jemma told her, sitting down on the floor with her. 'She's got the Barbie dreamhouse.'

'Oh, we've got that one too,' grinned Billie.

Whilst she and Billie were chatting, I made us all a cup of tea.

'Liz might have already told you, but I work for the police,' she told Billie. 'Maybe tomorrow after school would you like to come and see where I work?

'We've got a really big playroom with lots of toys in it, including some Barbies.

'You can have a drink and a biscuit and play with some toys and you and I can do some talking. Would that be OK?'

Billie nodded eagerly.

'I like biscuits and Barbies,' she said.

Thankfully Billie seemed to have really warmed to her.

'I've got to go now,' said Jemma. 'But I'm really looking forward to seeing you again tomorrow, Billie.'

Billie looked up.

'Bye,' she said, giving her a little wave.

Liz showed her out while I stayed with Billie.

'Well, she was a nice lady, wasn't she?' I said and she nodded.

I just hoped that she felt the same way the following day when Jemma started asking her difficult questions.

Later that night, Liz emailed me the details of the place where Billie would be being interviewed tomorrow. Sadly I already knew it well, as I'd been there several times in the past with various foster children. It was a safe house where children could be interviewed about the abuse they had suffered. The rooms were filled with special equipment to film what the children had to say, and it would sometimes be used as evidence in court. I knew the staff always did their best to put them at ease but it was somewhere I always dreading going because of what it represented, and that would never change.

The following day, I picked Billie up from school in the car.

'We're going to see Jemma now,' I told her. 'Remember the lady you met yesterday?'

'The one with the Barbies,' she nodded. 'Can I still have a biscuit?'

'Yes, I'm sure you can, sweetie,' I told her.

It was a thirty-minute drive to the building that I'd come to know as a safe house although I didn't know if that was its official name. It looked like a normal, new-build detached house in a quiet residential street.

'Is this the biscuit lady's house?' asked Billie as we knocked on the door.

'I know it looks like a house but it's actually where Jemma works,' I explained.

Jemma answered the door and took us into the kitchen at the front of the house. It looked like any other ordinary kitchen with a big table in the middle of it.

'Now let's get you that biscuit and some juice and then I'll show you the playroom.'

Billie wolfed down the biscuit and all four of us went upstairs. It was there that you could tell this was no ordinary house. Upstairs the bedrooms were set up as interview rooms. There was a room that we passed that I knew from previous visits was an examination room. There was a police doctor who could do internal examinations and take evidence. Thankfully Liz had already told me on this visit it was unlikely Billie would have to be examined, which I was relieved about. A physical examination was traumatic for any child, and particularly one as young as Billie.

'We know that if she has been abused then it's been in the past before she came to you,' Liz had told me. 'Which is two months ago.

'Depending on what Billie says, it might be something they want to do in the future, but there's not likely to be DNA or any injuries now.'

I followed Liz, Jemma and Billie down the landing to a big room at the front of the house.

'And this is the playroom,' Jemma told her. 'I've already got some things out that I thought you'd like.'

Billie shuffled over to the pile of Barbies and dolls that were set up on the floor.

It was a special purpose-built interview suite but it looked like a huge playroom.

'This is like the place I see Mummy, isn't it, Maggie?' said Billie, looking around and smiling.

'Yes, you're right, flower,' I smiled. 'It is a bit.'

Like the contact centre, the room was filled with squishy sofas, shelves of books and cupboards full of toys. The only difference here was the recording equipment set up discreetly in the corner.

I'd been here enough times to know the drill. As Billie's social worker, Liz would stay in the room while Jemma questioned her. I would go into an adjoining room where there was a desk with a monitor set up on it so I could see and hear what was being said next door.

'I'm just going to pop out and have a coffee while Jemma talks to you,' I told Billie, but she was so engrossed in the dolls, she didn't even look up.

I went into the monitor room and sat down. It was strange knowing that the conversation was happening just next door and yet I was seeing it unfold on screen. Anything that was recorded could eventually be used as evidence in court, so the police needed to make sure everything that took place followed proper procedure.

Liz sat on one of the sofas while Jemma sat on the floor with Billie. They chit-chatted about school and a few other things.

'Before you went to live at Maggie's, you used to live in another house, didn't you?' asked Jemma.

Billie nodded.

'Who lived in that house with you?'

'Mummy, Uncle Jim and Bo,' replied Billie.

'Did anyone else live there with you?'

Billie shook her head.

'Did any other grownups come round and visit you at your house?' she asked. 'Did Mummy or Uncle Jim have friends that might have popped in?'

Billie shook her head and carried on playing.

'Maggie was telling me about the tickling game that you used to play at home,' Jemma said. 'Who used to play that game?'

'Me and Bo Bo played it but she don't like it no more,' Billie told her sadly.

'Did anyone else play the tickling game with you?' Jemma asked her.

Billie shrugged.

'I don't know the tickling game,' Jemma told her. 'What happens in that game? Maybe you can show me using the dolls,' she suggested.

In amongst the Barbies there were two or three other dolls. Billie had taken the clothes off one of them and I could see it was anatomically correct.

Billie picked it up and sniggered.

'Look, this one's got a hole in its noo noo,' she grinned. 'The dolls at Maggie's don't have a hole.'

'Yes, that's right,' nodded Jemma. 'That one's a girl doll. Can you show me with that doll what the tickling game was?' She urged Billie gently.

Billie acted out what she'd told me when she and Bo had got out of the bath a few days earlier. Even though I knew what it involved, it was still horrifying to see her do it so casually, like she was showing us any other game.

'Maggie said that sometimes at home, you used to play the pokey pokey game as well,' said Jemma. 'Can you tell me a bit more about that one?'

Billie didn't even answer, she just tipped the doll upside down and rammed her finger in the hole.

'Or you can stick other things in there too,' she told Jemma matter-of-factly.

Jemma carried on with her questions.

'Billie, can you remember when you talked to Maggie and Liz the other day and you said that a grown up had taught you the tickling game. Who was that grown up?'

'Don't know,' she muttered.

'So who played the tickling game and the pokey pokey game with you?' asked Jemma gently.

'Bo Bo,' replied Billie.

'Did anyone else ever play those games with you, Billie? What about grown ups?' she asked. 'Are there any grown ups in your house who play those games too?'

Jemma was keeping things very simple and light. If you tell a child that someone's going to be in trouble for doing something then they're much more likely to be reluctant to say who it was.

'It's really important that you tell us who was playing these games with you,' Jemma told her. 'If you tell us then we can talk to them about it and ask them who taught them it.'

I watched the screen, my heart thumping.

Tell us, Billie, tell us.

I closed my eyes and waited to hear the name that I was expecting. But Billie suddenly yawned and put the doll down and started playing with the Barbies.

'Billie, who was the grown up who taught you the tickling game?' Jemma repeated.

Billie suddenly paused and looked up at her.

'I'm hungry,' she sighed. 'Can I have another biscuit? Or have you got any chocolate?'

I knew Billie well enough by then to know that, for whatever reason, she wasn't going to say any more.

Jemma tried a couple more times to get something more out of her but I knew it was no use.

Ten minutes later, they ended the interview.

'I'm sorry,' I told Jemma.

'It's so hard with kids. You never know what you're going to get,' she sighed. 'She did really well, poor girl. I'm sure that was a lot for her.

'We just need to know which adult or adults are responsible. We'll try again in a few days and in the meantime we'll speak to Mandy and Jim.'

They had to tread so carefully with children, especially when it came to something as traumatic as sexual abuse. They couldn't keep interviewing Billie for hours or repeat the same questions over and over again. It wasn't fair after everything she'd been through.

'Did you have a good play?' I asked Billie as I walked back into the room.

She nodded.

'I'm tired,' she said. 'Can we go home now, Maggie?'

'I know you are, flower,' I told her, putting my arm around her. 'Of course we can.'

It was my job to keep everything stable and normal and give Billie a break from the questions. So I focused on doing all the mundane stuff like making tea and letting her watch TV and giving her a bath.

That night, when we came home from the safe house, I'd deliberately planned a comforting dinner. We were having sausages and roast potatoes, which was Billie's favourite.

As I was peeling the potatoes, Billie came over to me.

'Can I help?' she asked. 'Will you show me how to peel the potatoes, Maggie?'

'If you're still living with me when you're a big girl then I'd be happy to teach you how to peel potatoes,' I smiled. 'But the peeler's a bit sharp and you're still too little at the moment.'

'But I *am* a big girl,' said Billie, looking annoyed. 'My Mummy said I was a big girl when she taught me the tickling game, so I am big enough to peel the potatoes.'

At first, I thought I'd misheard her. I put the peeler down on the work top.

'Say that again, lovey,' I asked her gently. 'Why are you a big girl?'

'Cos my Mummy said I was one,' she told me crossly. 'That's why she taught me the tickling game, so you see I *can* do potatoes.'

And just like that, over a sink full of potato peelings, we'd finally found out which grown up was responsible.

FOURTEEN

Victim to Monster

I was totally unprepared for what Billie had just told me.

Her own mother. How could anyone do that to their daughter?

I was absolutely horrified but I tried not to show Billie that.

'Dinner's not going to be ready for a little while yet, so why don't you have a play?' I told her, doing my best to keep my voice calm. 'I just need to go upstairs and make a quick phone call.'

My hands were shaking as I picked up my mobile and dialled Liz's number. It was 6 p.m., the end of her working day, and I prayed that she would answer.

Please pick up, please pick up . . .

'It's Mandy,' I gasped as soon as she answered. 'Liz, it's Mandy who's been doing it.'

'Maggie, are you OK?' she replied. 'It's Mandy who's been doing what?'

'It's Mandy who taught Billie the tickling game. She's the one who's been abusing her, not Jim.'

'What?' she gasped. 'How do you know?'

'Billie's just told me,' I replied. 'I was peeling some potatoes and she just came out with it. I suppose it was on her mind after all the questions from Jemma today.'

'Do you think she's telling you the truth?' Liz asked.

'I don't see why she wouldn't,' I shrugged.

'I don't know what to say,' she sighed. 'I'd got it into my head that Jim was the one who was abusing her. Poor Billie. Her own mother . . .'

I could hear the shock in her voice. I was annoyed at myself for making the same assumption. When we knew that it was likely Billie had been abused, I'd automatically questioned the men that had been around her and then pointed the finger at Jim. I'd never even considered Mandy. All sexual abuse was horrific, but nobody wanted to think of a mother sexually abusing her own daughter.

'What shall I do?' I asked Liz.

'There's nothing that we can do tonight,' she replied. 'I'll phone Jemma now and let her know what's happened.

'Then I assume they'll arrest Mandy, or at least bring her in for questioning.'

It wasn't long before Jemma phoned me. She was as stunned as Liz and I were. I went through what Billie had said to me and the exact wording that she'd used.

'Are you going to arrest Mandy?' I asked her.

'We'll need to talk to Billie again at the interview suite tomorrow first, just to check that she's still saying the same thing,' she replied.

'Do you want me to keep her off school?' I questioned.

'No, I think let's try and do it after school again and keep everything else as normal as possible for her,' she told me.

'I want to hear what Billie's saying before I question Mandy, and we'll probably need to speak to Jim too.'

As I walked downstairs to the kitchen, I took a deep breath to try and calm myself. Billie was still playing happily with the doll's house, oblivious to the panicked conversations going on upstairs.

My eyes filled with tears as I thought about what this poor girl had gone through at the hands of her own mother. It was just unspeakably horrific. But what was even more disturbing was the fact that she didn't know any different. She didn't understand that what Mandy had done to her was wrong.

I stuck to my original plan and tried to keep everything as normal and as calm as possible as I wanted her to have a good night's sleep. I also steered away from all conversation about the tickling game.

But, as I was tucking her into bed, it was Billie who brought it up.

'Will Mummy get into trouble for playing the tickling game with me?' she asked in a quiet voice. 'Will the police lady be cross with me?'

I sat on the bed next to her and put my hand on hers.

'I promise you, no one is going to be cross with you, Billie,' I told her. 'You've been so brave and I'm so glad that you told me.

'Jemma won't be cross but she'll probably want to talk to you about it.'

'How will Jemma know?' she asked.

'I will have to tell Liz and Jemma what you said,' I told her. 'Not because we're cross but because we all care about you and we want to make sure that you're OK, so it's important that they know everything. Is that OK?'

She shrugged.

I desperately wanted her to know that whatever happened over the next few days, none of this was her fault.

I didn't tell her about going back to the safe house until the next morning when she was eating breakfast.

'Jemma and Liz would really like to talk to you again,' I told her. 'So we're going to go and see them this afternoon.'

'At that place with the toys and the biscuits?' she asked, as she shovelled cereal into her mouth.

'Yes,' I nodded. 'We're going to go back there.'

Thankfully, Billie seemed fine about it and when I picked her up from school later that day, she was more interested in the biscuits that she was going to have when we got there.

I went back into the monitor room next door while Jemma and Liz sat in the interview suite with Billie.

'So what did you do when you went home last night?' Jemma asked her casually as Billie played.

'Umm, I watched telly and we had our tea,' muttered Billie as she roughly combed a Barbie's hair.

'What did you have for tea?'

'Sausages and roast potatoes,' replied Billie.

'That sounds lovely,' smiled Jemma. 'I like roast potatoes but I don't like peeling them.'

She paused.

'Who peels the potatoes in Maggie's house?'

'Maggie does,' replied Billie. 'But she says that when I'm a big girl that she'll show me how to peel them.'

'So do you think that you're a big girl now?' Jemma asked her.

Billie nodded firmly. I fiddled nervously with my watch-strap, wondering whether she was going to repeat what she said to me last night.

'But you're only seven,' smiled Jemma. 'Are you sure you're a big girl?'

I could see Billie was getting a little bit annoyed now.

'I *am* a big girl cos my mummy taught me the tickling game and she says only big girls can play it.'

Relief flooded my body and I sank back into the hard office chair that I was perched on. She'd repeated the same allegation, and this time, they'd got it on tape.

Liz and Jemma looked at each other.

'So did Mummy just play the tickling game with you?' asked Jemma. 'Or did she play it with anyone else?'

Billie shook her head.

'She just played it with me cos I'm a big girl. Bo Bo's too little.'

'When did you play the game with Mummy?'

'A lot of times,' Billie told her. 'When Uncle Jim was away Mummy let me sleep in her bed. And sometimes I played it with Bo cos that's what you do when you love somebody.'

Her words made me shudder.

That's what you do when you love somebody.

That was obviously what Mandy had told her and what the poor little mite had come to believe.

Billie was still so calm, and she wasn't getting at all upset with the questions, which made my heart break even more. The sad fact was that this abuse was a normal part of her day-to-day life.

While Billie played in the room with Jemma, Liz and I popped downstairs to the kitchen to make everyone a drink.

'It was heartbreaking to hear her say that,' sighed Liz. 'I wonder what Mandy's going to say about it all.'

'What are we going to do about contact?' I asked her.

Billie and Bo were next due to see their mum at the contact centre in a couple of days.

Even though contact was supervised, Mandy could talk to the girls about the police investigation or manipulate them, and Social Services wouldn't want to take the risk.

'I'll seek advice from my managers and our legal team, but I think this week's sessions definitely won't happen,' Liz told me. 'They might restart again after she's been questioned.'

Mandy still had a right to see her children and in the eyes of the law, she was innocent until proven guilty.

In the meantime, I made sure that life carried on as normal as it could for Billie. Even though they weren't seeing Mandy, she and Bo could still see each other, and I knew it was important for Billie to see her sister, so we arranged for us to go round to Angela's the following day after school. I thought it was better to do that than invite Bo round to our house as I didn't want to upset her and make her think that she was coming back.

'Mummy's busy talking to Jemma today so we're going to go and see Bo at her new house instead of going to the contact centre,' I told her.

Billie was ecstatic, as it meant that she could see Ziggy the dog. As soon as we arrived, both girls went out into the garden with him and we kept an eye on them through the open patio doors.

'It sounds like it's been a stressful few days,' Angela smiled sympathetically as she made me a cup of tea.

'Poor Billie,' I sighed. 'She's just as much a victim as Bo in all this. God knows what went on in that house.'

Angela explained that Jemma had been round to have an informal chat with Bo too.

'From what Bo said, thankfully it doesn't sound as if Mum did anything to her,' she told me.

Jemma had already texted me that morning to say that they were questioning Mandy today. She'd said it might be a few days before she got back to us with an update as they were hoping to get a statement from Jim too.

The following day, Liz and I had a meeting at Billie's school with the head teacher, Mrs Moody, and her class teacher, Miss Senior. They wanted to discuss the safeguarding measures that they needed to put in place since we'd discovered that Billie had been abusing Bo.

Liz had already filled them in on the developments with Mum and they knew that Billie had been interviewed by the police. It was important for the school to be aware of what was going in Billie's life, especially with serious allegations like this. If she got upset at school or said something to her teachers, then they needed to know the whole picture and what she was going through.

'There's no indication at all that Billie would abuse another child but, as I'm sure you're aware, for safeguarding reasons we have to put these measures in,' Liz told them. 'They're designed not only to protect other children but Billie as well.'

It meant that Billie wasn't allowed to be alone unsupervised with any other pupils. She couldn't go to the toilet on her own – a member of staff would always have to go with her – and they had to keep a close watch on her when they were getting changed for PE in the classroom.

'Logistically, it's a huge amount of work,' sighed Mrs Moody. 'A member of staff has to have their eyes on Billie all of the time. Even at playtime she has to be continually watched. The lunchtime supervisors have been taking it in turns but it's quite a challenge for one person to have her in sight all the time in a busy playground.'

'I appreciate that,' nodded Liz. 'But it's something that has to be done.'

Mrs Moody had always been incredibly accommodating and understanding when it came to issues that I'd had with foster children in the past, but today she seemed flustered and panicked. I understood that it was hard work for the school, but Billie was a victim too and to keep everyone safe, this was what needed to be done.

'Do you think I should move her to the other side of the classroom away from other children?' asked Miss Senior, a worried look on her face. 'It would be easier to keep an eye on her that way.'

'I don't think anything as extreme as that is necessary,' Liz explained.

As Liz talked them through all the safeguarding measures, Mrs Moody frowned.

'As a perpetrator of abuse, do you really think this is the right school for Billie?' she asked. 'Do you think she might be better off going somewhere more secure that's geared up for this level of supervision?'

I'd been biting my tongue for the past few minutes but I couldn't keep quiet any longer.

'At the end of the day, I think it's important to remember we're talking about a seven-year-old girl here who has suffered a huge amount of abuse herself,' I told them, politely but firmly. 'Billie has never tried to harm or abuse another child outside of her own home and there's no suggestion that she would.

'She's been through enough in her short life,' I sighed. 'I don't want her to feel any more isolated than she already is. It's as much about keeping her safe as it is the other children. She's a victim too in all of this.'

I could see Mrs Moody was taken aback.

'I understand, Maggie,' she nodded. 'It's just a lot to take on.'

By the end of the meeting, I was feeling quite irritated. What Billie needed most right now was love and support and to feel included rather than feeling as though she was being isolated, punished and shamed. I knew it was tricky for the school with limited resources but it was something that had to be done.

'I thought they'd be a little bit more understanding,' I said to Liz on the way out. 'Particularly after what's happened in the past couple of days. She's a seven-year-old girl, not a monster.'

Thankfully Billie seemed fine about it all. That afternoon, she came home from school all excited.

'You look like you've had a good day,' I said as she came out of the classroom smiling from ear to ear.

She thrust an envelope into my hand.

'Lola's invited me to her birthday party,' she grinned. 'She's having a sleepover and there's gonna be popcorn and birthday cake.'

My heart immediately sank. I knew there was no way Billie would be able to go. She wouldn't be allowed to share a bedroom with three other girls unsupervised overnight.

'I'm so sorry, sweetie, but you can't go,' I told her. 'Because you're in care, if you go and stay at someone's house then they have to have special police checks. I've got one but Lola's mummy and daddy don't.'

'But can they get one?' she asked, her tears filling her eyes.

I shook my head.

'There's not enough time, flower, and it's a lot more complicated than that.'

Police checks were a convenient and legitimate excuse for why she couldn't go, but in truth, there was no way that Billie would be allowed to go to any sleepover, given the abuse allegations. If she did, I would have to tell Lola's parents about her past history and I didn't want to do that at the risk of her being shunned. It was important to protect Billie as much as possible.

I called Lola's mum, who was called Lisa, and explained the situation.

'I feel bad that she's missing out,' she sighed. 'If Billie can't come to the sleepover then why doesn't she just come for the afternoon and then she can go home before bedtime?'

'I'm sure she would love that,' I told her, feeling relieved.

I hesitated.

'Would it be possible for me to come along too?' I asked.

'Oh . . . er, yes, I suppose that's fine if you'd like to,' she replied, sounding surprised.

I didn't want to deprive Billie of doing normal things any seven-year-old would do but I needed to make sure that I was there to watch her at all times when she was around other children. That way I wouldn't have to disclose any information to the other parents.

I did feel awkward, and it was embarrassing inviting myself along to someone's house that I didn't know. But I was prepared to put my discomfort to one side so Billie didn't miss out.

Lola's mum was actually very nice. I explained that I always had to keep a close eye on Billie and be in the same room as her.

'It's all to do with duty of care,' I explained.

I could see that she thought it was a bit odd but it was better than telling her the real reason.

When the girls watched a film in the living room, I sat with them. When they ran upstairs, laughing and giggling, to Lola's bedroom, I had to follow them up there too.

I was trying to be as discreet as I could so Billie didn't feel embarrassed around her friends. I made sure the bedroom door was open and I perched on the top of the stairs.

'Why is your mum sat on the stairs spying on us?' I heard Lola say.

'She isn't my mum,' snapped Billie. 'She's Maggie and she just has to check on me.'

'Why?' giggled one of the other girls, who was called Sienna. 'What have you done?'

'I haven't done anything,' said Billie, getting upset.

'You must be really naughty,' teased Lola. 'Even when you go to the toilet at school, miss always comes with you.'

'No she doesn't,' snapped Billie.

Billie had already missed out on so much of her childhood and I desperately wanted her to have a normal life. But her past was always coming back and making that impossible.

FIFTEEN

Teaching and Learning

'Do you think a child like Billie has got the ability to change?' asked my friend Vicky as she took a gulp of tea. 'Or do you think she'll always be a risk to other children?'

'I don't think she's going to be a risk in the long term. I think with the right help and support she can change,' I nodded. 'I believe that one hundred per cent.'

While Billie was at school, Vicky had come round for a chat. It felt good to talk to someone about what had been going on over the past few days.

'It must be such a difficult situation,' she told me. 'I've never fostered a child who has abused another child before.'

'I know it sounds awful, but I do feel as though I have to keep reminding everyone that we're talking about a seven-year-old girl here who's also been abused,' I sighed. 'What she was doing to Bo was terrible, but she didn't know or understand that. Sexual abuse was a normal part of her life, something she'd experienced for as long as she could remember, and she didn't know any different. It's learned behaviour.

'It's not about excluding her or shaming her, it's about re-teaching her.'

I knew how important it was to give Billie the knowledge that this wasn't what adults did to children and it wasn't what children did to other children either.

Vicky still looked a little sceptical.

'It's a bit like this,' I told Vicky. 'Imagine if, for all your life, what other people called a milk jug, you called a turnip.'

Vicky laughed.

'What are you on about, Maggie?'

'Bear with me,' I smiled. 'You know how I love a good analogy. So, you firmly believe that a milk jug is called a turnip,' I continued. 'Then, suddenly, you come to my house and I ask you to pass me the milk jug. You'd think, what's she on about? That's a turnip.

'That's what's happening for Billie right now. She's feeling complete and utter confusion as everyone is telling her that everything that she's ever known in her life is wrong.'

The fact was that ever since she'd been taken into care, we'd turned Billie's world upside down. My house was odd to her from the get go because it wasn't her house, and she didn't have her mum and uncle around. The fact that at night she had a bath, put on her pyjamas and went to bed at a set time was strange. The fact that she had to sit down for meals and wasn't supposed to poo and wee on the floor any more was odd in her eyes. We'd questioned most of the things she'd done for the first seven years of her life. The abuse was something that she had been doing and had been done to her for much of her life. Now everyone was telling her that that was wrong too.

'In the past few months, she's learned how to change all of those things and adapt to new ways,' I told Vicky. 'I'm confident she can do the same with the abuse.

'It's just about explaining to her that it's wrong and that it hurts people.'

'Therapy will help her understand that too,' nodded Vicky.

'It will,' I sighed. 'When it finally happens.'

Billie and Bo had been referred to have play therapy, which we'd all agreed would be best for them, based on their age, but sadly there was such a demand for it that the waiting list was endless. Liz said it might be months before a space came up.

So, while the police investigation was going on in the background, I did my own work with Billie to try and help her understand and make sense of what had happened to her.

'How does it feel when Liz, Jemma or I talk to you about the tickling game?' I asked her one day, whilst we were doing some colouring in together.

I'd often found that it was easier to talk to children about difficult subjects whilst they were distracted by another activity and didn't have to make eye contact.

Billie shook her head, focusing on the flower she was colouring in.

'Don't know,' she sighed.

'Does it make you feel happy or excited? I asked.

She shook her head.

'What about scared or sad?'

She shrugged her shoulders.

'It makes me feel a bit sicky in my tummy and my head feels all muddly.'

'Muddly is a really good word,' I smiled.

174

To me, a muddle was something had made her confused and scared, but it was also a word without blame.

It was so important for Billie to understand that the tickling game caused lots of muddles inside her and it had caused Bo lots of muddles too. Once Billie recognised her own muddles, she'd see how they affected other children.

Liz came round one afternoon to see how we were getting on. I'd already had a chat with her about the work we'd been doing around muddles. Billie was playing on the floor over the other side of the kitchen.

'How are you, Maggie?' Liz asked me. 'How have you been getting on?'

'Billie and I have been doing lots of talking,' I told her loudly. 'We've been chatting about the tickling game and all the muddles Billie has been feeling.'

Liz nodded, aware that I was hoping that Billie would hear what we were saying.

'And are you cross at Billie for playing the tickling game, Maggie?' Liz asked.

Billie stopped playing and froze, and I could see her suddenly tune into our conversation.

'I'm sad that Billie didn't listen to her sister when Bo was saying that she didn't want to play the tickling game. But I'm not cross with Billie at all, because she was taught that game by her mummy and she didn't know it wasn't something that you should do to other people.'

Obviously intrigued, Billie wandered over to me and put her hand on my knee. She looked up at me with her big blue eyes.

'Are you cross with my mummy, Maggie?'

Normally I went out of my way to not speak negatively about birth parents in front of their children, but this was an entirely different situation. Billie needed to clearly understand that what Mandy had done to her was very wrong.

'I'm afraid I am very cross with your mummy, yes,' I told her. 'Because mummies shouldn't teach their children that sort of a game.'

'What do you think, Liz?' I asked. 'Are you cross with Billie's mummy?'

'I am,' she nodded. 'The tickling game isn't a game mummies and children should play together and it's caused you a lot of muddles, hasn't it?'

Billie nodded sadly.

During our conversations, I also talked to Billie about bodies and the fact that certain parts of our body were private and nobody should touch them except us. I used the idea of safe and unsafe touching. I wanted Billie to know that some touching was perfectly OK.

'So, at night, if you're going to bed and I give you a hug, that's safe touching,' I told her. 'It's not hurting you and I've asked you if you'd like a hug, and we've both got our clothes on.

'Or if you hold hands with your friend Lola at school. That's safe touching because you're just being friendly and Lola's happy for you to hold her hand when you're playing and it doesn't hurt her.'

I'd talk to her as often as I could about it to make it a normal part of her day to day. One night she was in the bath and I was washing her hair.

'What kind of touching am I doing now, Billie?' I asked her as I rinsed out the shampoo.

'Safe touching,' Billie told me instantly.

'That's right,' I smiled. 'And what wouldn't be safe touching?'

'If you touched my noo noo,' she replied. 'Cos it's my noo noo and nobody else's.'

'That's absolutely right,' I smiled, pleased that what we'd been talking about was sinking in.

My agency provided me with body sheets to mark where children had injuries or cuts and bruises like the kind I'd filled in when Billie and Bo had first come to live with me. We used some spare ones to mark which places were acceptable to do safe touching.

Billie drew a picture of a hairbrush next to the top of the head.

'Cos brushing hair is a good touch, isn't it, Maggie?' she told me.

Then she drew a cross on the arms.

'Cos a cuddle is a safe touch.'

However, at the same time as all of this, I wanted her to understand that there was nothing wrong with touching her own body. She just needed to do it in private, safe places like the bathroom or her bedroom. I didn't want her growing up being ashamed of touching her own body. It was a tricky balance, especially with a seven-year-old child, but all I could do was keeping talking to her about it and be open with her.

A few nights later, Louisa called in after work. Billie was playing in the kitchen while I made fish pie for tea. Louisa looked shocked when she saw Billie.

'Gosh, she's lost so much weight,' she whispered to me. 'I haven't seen her for a few weeks and she looks like a different girl.'

'Does she?' I replied. 'I suppose she has. I don't tend to notice as much when I see her every day.'

My head had been so full of other things for the past few weeks, I hadn't even noticed her weight loss, although I'd had to tighten the waistband on some of her clothes recently.

When we'd gone round to Angela's, I'd been struck by how Bo was a lot slimmer too. In fact, both of the girls had been tearing around the garden with Ziggy and it had been lovely to see them running around like other children their age without gasping for breath.

'And how are you feeling, lovey?' I asked gently, pointing to Louisa's growing bump. 'You've really popped out in the last few days,' I smiled. 'There's no mistaking there's a baby in there now. You're blooming.'

Louisa grinned and patted her stomach.

'She's been moving around like crazy too,' she smiled. 'It's really reassuring to feel her wriggling around, apart from when she does cartwheels at night when I'm trying to sleep.'

'Would you mind if I had a feel?' I asked her. 'I'd love to be able to feel her kicking.'

'Normally, I hate people touching my bump, but I think I can make an exception when it comes to her nana,' she told me, grinning. 'Although, just to warn you, she might not play ball.'

I held my hands out and gently placed them on Louisa's stomach,

'No!' Billie suddenly shouted from where she was playing, her eyes wide.

She got up and came running over to us.

'No, Maggie,' she scolded. 'You can't do that. That's not safe touching.'

Louisa looked at me with a puzzled expression on her face.

'It's OK, sweetie,' I gently explained to Billie. 'I asked Louisa if I could touch her bump to feel the baby kicking and Louisa has all her clothes on and she knows that it's not going to hurt her.'

Billie considered this for a moment, but then she looked satisfied, and settled back down to play.

Louisa looked well and truly confused by now.

'What was all that about?' she asked in a low voice. 'Of course I've got my clothes on.'

'Oh, it's just some work we've been doing about bodies,' I told her vaguely.

For confidentiality reasons, I hadn't told Louisa what had been going on, and she seemed to accept this without question. It was good to know that what I'd been talking about with Billie was slowly sinking in.

'Can Charlie and I pop in for a cup of tea one night this week?' she asked me. 'I feel like we haven't caught up properly for ages.'

'Of course you can, flower,' I told her. 'Why don't you come later on one evening when Billie's in bed?'

I felt bad that I'd not had as much time with Louisa as usual as I was always a little bit distracted and focused on Billie when she was around.

Louisa kept to her word, and she and Charlie popped round the following evening. We talked about their work, the decorating they'd been doing on their flat as well as talking about the baby, and it was good to see that Louisa seemed happier to talk about her a bit more now.

'We even started to do a few bits to the nursery the other day,' she told me. 'I wanted to make it a little bit more girly for her so we painted the drawers pink and I bought a little pink teddy bear.'

'That sounds lovely,' I smiled.

I was glad that she was finally allowing herself to get excited. For months after Dominic died, Louisa couldn't even bring herself to go into that room and she'd kept the door shut.

'That's actually what we wanted to come round and talk to you about, Maggie,' said Charlie. 'Would you mind if we started getting a few of the baby things down from your loft?'

'Not all, flower,' I told him. 'They're all your things for you to get whenever you want. I was just storing them for you.'

'We just wanted a few things like the pram you bought us and the Moses basket,' nodded Louisa. 'It feels nice to be able to use some of Dominic's things for his little sister.'

'Of course,' I told her, giving her hand a squeeze. 'In fact, you can go up now, Charlie, if you want and get some of the stuff down.

'Remember, Billie's in bed so try not to make too much noise.'

While Charlie went upstairs to go into the loft hatch, I made Louisa and myself another cup of tea.

'I'm glad that you're getting excited about the baby, lovey,' I told her.

'Sometimes I feel so guilty though, Maggie,' she sighed. 'I allow myself to feel happy but then it feels like I'm betraying Dominic.

'Even though we're having another baby, I'll never forget him, you know,' she said, tears filling her eyes. 'I'll miss him for ever.'

'Of course you won't forget him, Louisa,' I told her gently. 'He's always going to be your son. You can still feel happy and sad at the same time.'

This new baby wasn't going to instantly take Louisa's grief away. In fact, in many ways, it might make her loss more painful and raw as she realised what she had missed out on with Dominic.

'I'm really worried that being in the same hospital will bring it all back,' she told me. 'When I go there for scans, all I can think about is holding him for the last time.

'I remember how it felt to be walking out of that hospital knowing I was never going to see him again. The only thing in my arms was a memory box.'

Her lip trembled and tears spilled down her face.

'Oh, flower,' I said. 'I can only imagine how tough this must be for you, but you will get through it.'

I was giving her a hug when Charlie walked back in.

'I've put the Moses basket and the pram in the hall,' he told us.

He put a couple of cardboard boxes down on the floor.

'I think these are some of the blankets and clothes that you wanted,' he told Louisa.

She opened one of the boxes and there was a little white cardigan with a blue trim on the top. Louisa picked it up and held it to her chest.

'Oh, I remember this,' she sighed. 'It's one of the first ones you knitted for us, Maggie.'

'I did get a bit overexcited,' I smiled.

'No, it's lovely that we've already got all this stuff,' she said.

'Why don't I change the buttons on it?' I suggested. 'I could put some little blue flower-shaped buttons on it.'

'That would be lovely,' nodded Louisa, wiping away her tears.

As Charlie loaded up the car, I gave her another big hug.

'I know this is so hard for you but it's going to be OK,' I reassured her. 'Having another baby is going to bring up all sorts of new feelings and grief for you both, but just make sure you keep talking about it, OK? I'm always here for you, lovey,'

She nodded bravely.

'Thanks, Maggie.'

Keep talking. That's all she could do and that's all I was doing with Billie too.

One morning before school, Billie was playing with the doll's house and the Barbies.

'Maggie, this is my old house,' she told me.

I was a little taken aback, as she rarely talked about her old house any more, but I knew it was just important to go along with it.

'Your old house where you used to live with Mummy?' I asked her and she nodded.

I went and sat down beside her on the floor as I thought this could be another opportunity to reinforce all of the things that we'd been discussing over the past few days.

'Who are these dollies then?' I asked her, picking up the Barbies.

'This one is Bo,' Billie said, pulling one of them out of my hands. 'And she's going to bed now.'

'Let's put Bo in her bed then,' I told her. 'Show me where she sleeps.'

'Night night, Bo Bo,' said Billie, giving the doll a kiss on the forehead before laying her down in one of the beds.

Then she picked up another Barbie.

'This one's Billie,' she told me.

'Oh hello, Billie, it's very nice to meet you,' I said, pretending to talk to the doll, and Billie giggled.

'Let's put Billie in her bed then,' I replied. 'Which bed is she going to sleep in?'

'This one,' she said, pointing to another bed in a different room. 'Cos sisters sleep in their own beds, don't they, Maggie?'

'That's absolutely right, lovey,' I smiled.

'Now it's Mummy's turn,' said Billie, picking up another Barbie.

I was pleased when she put it in another bed in a different room.

'Night night, Mummy,' I added, watching her tuck the doll in.

'And who's this doll?' I asked, pointing at the last Barbie.

'That's Uncle Jim,' smiled Billie.

'Ooh, I didn't know Uncle Jim wore a pink dress,' I joked and Billie giggled.

'Let's put Uncle Jim to bed then,' I added.

As Billie was doing that, I walked over to load the last few breakfast dishes into the dishwasher. When I came back, I noticed she'd put the doll on top of the mummy doll in the same bed.

'That's a bit silly,' I smiled. 'You've put Uncle Jim in Mummy's bed.

'Where does he really sleep?' I asked her, lifting the doll out. 'We need to put him in his own bed in his bedroom.'

'No, that's right, Maggie,' Billie told me firmly.

She grabbed the doll from my hand and put it back into the bed where the 'mummy' Barbie was.

'Uncle Jim sleeps in that bed with Mummy.'

I felt a shiver run down my spine. I was about to ask a question I didn't think I wanted to know the answer to.

'Billie, in your real house, where does Uncle Jim sleep?' I asked her. 'Are you just pretending that they sleep in the same bed?'

Billie threw the doll down on the floor and I could see that she was annoyed.

'I'm not pretending,' she said, tears of anger in her eyes. 'That's Mummy and Uncle Jim's bed and that's where they always sleep in my house so don't move him.'

And just like that, just when I thought we'd discovered all there was to know about what Billie had been through, another bombshell was dropped that made us question everything all over again.

SIXTEEN

Family Values

I was becoming an expert at keeping a deadpan expression on my face even if inside I was overwhelmed by sheer panic. I dropped Billie off at school that morning and as soon as I was back in the safety of my car, I phoned Liz.

'Surely she was joking or just playing around?' she asked me when I told her what Billie had said.

'I honestly don't think so,' I replied. 'She got quite cross when I suggested that.'

'Are Mandy and Jim definitely blood brother and sister?' I asked, dreading the answer.

'That was what they've always led us to believe,' she told me. 'And I don't see why they'd have said that if it wasn't true.'

Hopefully it was all just a misunderstanding. After all, the alternative didn't bear thinking about.

'Did you visit the house?' I asked Liz.

'Yes, I went over there when the girls both first came into care but I didn't see every room and I didn't check who slept where,' she told me.

'Funnily enough, Bo said something to Angela a while ago about Uncle Jim and Mummy's bedroom but Angela thought she was just getting confused.'

As Billie might say, it was all one enormous muddle.

'I need to talk to Mandy again, as well as Jim,' sighed Liz. 'It might be a big mix-up or it could be that they didn't have another bedroom so they were forced to share.

'It might not mean what we're thinking. There could be a simple explanation.

'But I will have to pass this information on to Jemma too, as incest, if that's what this is, is illegal.'

Liz called back later that day to say the police wanted to deal with it directly.

'Jemma thinks it's best if they question Mandy and Jim first, before Social Services, to see if they think there's grounds for a criminal investigation,' she told me.

All we could do was sit and wait.

It was three long days before we had any updates.

'Jemma wants to come round to your house this morning and talk to us both,' Liz told me on the phone.

'That's absolutely fine,' I replied. 'Did she give you any indication of what she might say?'

'Nothing,' she sighed. 'Your guess is as good as mine.'

Billie was at school so we could talk freely. When everyone had arrived, I made us all a cup of tea and we sat round the kitchen table.

'Well, we've spent the past few days questioning Mandy and we've also spoken to Jim,' Jemma told us.

'And?' I asked nervously. 'What did Mandy say about the tickling game and what she'd done to Billie?'

Jemma shrugged her shoulders.

'We couldn't get anything out of her,' she sighed. 'Not a single thing.

'We told her what Billie had alleged and she just got very giggly and said that she didn't know.

'To be honest, it was like talking to a child, not a grown woman. She just comes across as extremely naïve.'

She described how they had also questioned Jim.

'Because of his job, he was away three or four nights a week and he's adamant that he doesn't know anything about Mandy abusing Billie or any of these games,' she told us.

'What does that mean in terms of charging her?' asked Liz.

'All we have is Mum's word against Billie's,' said Jemma. 'Also because of Mandy's learning difficulties, I'm not sure whether she even has the mental capacity to be tried in court. 'That would be something the Crown would have to decide.'

She explained that they'd passed the file on to the Crown Prosecution Service (CPS), who would make a decision whether to charge Mandy with anything. They would decide whether it was worth pursuing the case on the basis of whether there was likely to be a conviction.

'And then, of course, we have the latest allegations of incest,' Jemma told us. 'Mandy was a lot more forthcoming about that.'

I couldn't hide the horrified expression on my face as Jemma revealed how Mandy had freely admitted to being in a sexual relationship with Jim for a number of years.

'She was very open about it,' Jemma told us. 'In fact, it was almost as though she couldn't see that there was anything wrong with it.'

It was all desperately sad. I was getting the sense that Mandy was as much a victim as Billie and Bo were.

'I think we also need to prepare ourselves for the distinct possibility that Jim is the father of both girls,' she added.

'What?' I gasped, completely taken aback.

Liz nearly spat out her tea.

'Mandy virtually said as much during our interview with her, but we will of course need to clarify this.'

My heart broke for Billie and Bo and the dysfunctional family that they'd been born into. They'd already been through so much and now potentially they were going to have to cope with being told that their uncle was actually their father.

'We'll need to establish if what she's implying is true by doing a DNA test on the girls,' said Jemma.

'The girls get their blood taken every month to check their vitamin D levels,' I told her. 'In fact, they're due to go back to the hospital next week. Could you use that?'

'Normally we'd do a mouth swab to obtain their cheek cells, but if they're used to doing the blood test then we could look at testing that,' nodded Jemma.

'What did Jim say about it when you questioned him?' asked Liz.

'He was extremely angry,' Jemma replied. 'He denied everything and said that Mandy was stupid, sick in the head and making it all up.'

He'd refused point blank to give them a DNA sample.

'I'm going to go back to him again and request that he co-operates with us,' Jemma said. 'If he doesn't, then we can apply to the courts for an order to force him to provide one.'

It was all just one big mess.

'Where on earth do we go from here?' I asked Liz after Jemma had gone. My head was spinning after everything we'd just learned.

'Regardless of the criminal proceedings, I think Social Services have got some big decisions to make when it comes to the long-term future of the girls,' she replied.

I knew she was right, and my heart broke all over again for Billie and Bo. They were the ultimate victims in all this. They were both just little girls, with no say or understanding of the world they had been born into.

A few days later, Liz scheduled another LAC review. This time, because of the ongoing police investigations, Mandy and Jim weren't invited, so the meeting was held at my house. Liz was coming along, as well as Becky, Angela and the girls' IRO, Michelle.

'I've had a look through all the information from the police,' sighed Michelle. 'It just beggars belief.'

She asked Liz what her thoughts were.

'I've been talking to my managers and, regardless of whether the CPS decide to pursue any criminal charges, I think Social Services have decided to go for a full care order for the girls,' she said. 'I don't think they can go back to Mum.

'It's becoming increasingly clear to us that Mandy isn't able to keep Billie and Bo safe and we're not sure that she has the mental capacity to parent, even with the right support.'

I nodded along in agreement. It was sad but true, and I felt like it was the right decision all round.

I knew from experience, though, that a full care order could often take six months or more to go through the courts.

'So whilst that's happening we need to think about a long-term solution for both girls,' Michelle told us.

'Could Bo and Billie potentially live together again?' she asked. 'Is that something we could look at?'

'I don't know how you feel about it, Maggie,' replied Liz. 'But my view is that it's too soon.'

'I totally agree,' I nodded. 'Billie has made some amazing progress but I think she's still understanding and learning, and you can't put a time limit on that.'

With sexual abuse, there was often a trigger, and perhaps Bo was Billie's trigger. At times of stress or upset for children, it can often make them revert back to previous behaviours. If Billie moved back in with Bo then it could possibly re-trigger the abuse.

Michelle nodded.

'As I've said to Liz, I'm more than happy to keep Bo on long-term,' said Angela.

She'd described how she'd settled in really well.

'She gets on well with the boys and she's hopefully starting pre-school soon,' she told us. 'She's a really sweet little girl and she's come on leaps and bounds.'

'So, Angela is happy to keep Bo on long-term,' said Michelle. 'So I suppose it's just a case of whether you could have Billie long-term too, Maggie. Is that something you would consider?'

My stomach sank. I didn't know what to say.

'I – I'll, er, have a think about it,' I stammered.

Becky and I exchanged looks, and I knew she understood what I was thinking.

'Maggie and I will have a chat about it after the meeting and feed back to Liz,' Becky told her firmly, and I was relieved not to have to give an answer there and then.

When everyone else had left, I collapsed into the sofa, my heart heavy.

'I didn't know what to say,' I sighed. 'Michelle really put me on the spot there.'

'I'm sorry about that, Maggie,' sympathised Becky. 'I really felt for you.'

We both knew what the implications would be if I kept Billie on long-term. Because she had abused another child, I wouldn't be able to foster any other children while she was in my care. Even with an older child, I'd seen how hard it was when Billie was here to keep an eye her at all times. It just wasn't manageable, especially as a single carer.

'I'm so fond of Billie,' I sighed. 'And she's been through so much. She's come such a long way in the time that she's been here, but if I have her long-term it's going to seriously limit my fostering going forwards.'

The reason I'd gone into fostering in the first place was to help as many children as I could. Billie was only seven, and realistically she could be with me for another ten or eleven years yet.

'I'm always happy to consider taking children on in the long-term,' I sighed. 'I mean, I had Louisa for all those years. But with Billie, it would mean I was effectively ending my career.'

'I completely understand,' nodded Becky. 'And there's also the implications with Louisa's new baby to think about.'

The harsh reality suddenly hit me.

'I hadn't even thought of that,' I gasped.

If I was fostering Billie, I wouldn't be able to have the baby in the house or to stay overnight. I thoroughly believed that Billie could be rehabilitated, and she hadn't shown any abusive behaviour towards any other child since Bo. But I couldn't guarantee with one hundred per cent certainty that she wouldn't do it again. Was I really willing to risk the safety of my own grandchild? It would also mean that I would have to tell Louisa about Billie's background and I didn't think she would want her daughter in the house. She wouldn't want to take the risk.

After everything that had happened with Dominic, all the tears and the grief, this was such a wanted baby and I was so looking forward to helping Louisa and spending time getting to know my new grandchild.

'I couldn't do that to Louisa,' I sighed. 'She's going to need a lot of support when this baby comes. I want to be there for her, and selfishly, I want to be able to help look after my granddaughter and have her to stay here.

'I couldn't do that if Billie was around.'

Billie could be rehabilitated but we didn't know when that might be. It certainly wasn't going to be by the time Louisa's baby was due. Three months wasn't long enough for a child to get over a lifetime of abuse and dysfunction.

Even though I knew it was ultimately the right decision for me, I felt devastated.

'How can I say no?' I said, the tears starting to spill down my cheeks. 'I can't let Billie down like that.

'There's a seven-year-old girl who's been through hell and who needs me, and now I'm putting her through more upheaval and rejection.'

I felt so selfish.

'Maggie, you've done everything you possibly can for Billie,' Becky told me. 'Look how far she's come since she's been with you. You fought so hard to keep her and you've laid the foundations for her future. Another carer could carry on the good work that you've done.'

'I know,' I sobbed. 'I just feel so guilty.'

'You're being too hard on yourself,' Becky soothed. 'You have a right to have a life of your own.

'This would limit your fostering and it would stop you being able to care for your own grandchild.'

'I know,' I nodded. 'I can't imagine not being able to have them to stay or have them in the house. I couldn't do that to Louisa or myself.'

It still didn't make it any easier though.

'I'll explain everything to Liz,' Becky reassured me. 'She will completely understand why you don't feel like you can do this, Maggie.'

It was an impossible situation. I knew I was making the right choice for me but I was overwhelmed with guilt and I felt as though I was letting Billie down.

Now we knew the girls weren't going to go back and live with Mandy, we had to tell them. Liz and I talked about it and we decided not to tell Billie that she wasn't staying with me until we could tell her about the carer that she was going to live with.

'It's too much uncertainty for her to cope with,' said Liz, and I agreed.

Liz came round one afternoon after school to talk to Billie. She arrived just as she was having a drink and a snack at the table.

'Maggie and I wanted to have a chat to you, Billie,' she told her.

Billie rolled her eyes.

'Not more talking,' she sighed.

'I know talking can feel really boring sometimes but this is important,' Liz told her, and I nodded in agreement.

'So I went to see a judge and I told her all about you and Bo and she's decided that it's best if you don't go back and live with Mummy,' she told her.

Billie didn't say anything but I could see her little mind taking it all in.

'Is that because Mummy was naughty?' Billie asked.

'It's because she made some bad choices,' I said.

'You're still going to see Mummy, though,' Liz reassured her. 'You can still go and visit her at the contact centre.'

Social Services had already decided that, over the next few weeks, they'd gradually reduce the number of contacts Mandy had with the girls. Billie and Bo were used to having two sessions a week so the sessions would gradually reduce to once a week for a couple of weeks, then once a fortnight for a month or so, then it would peter out until it was three times a year. It wasn't set in stone and it didn't always have to be that way. As children got older and developed more of an understanding, they could request to see their birth parents more. There also wouldn't be the need for a big goodbye session with Mandy because they were still going to see her. It might all need to change again in the future depending on if there was a court case. But, for now, Mandy was still able to see her children.

'So you'll still see Mummy and Uncle Jim if you want to, just not as much,' Liz told her.

'What about Bo?' asked Billie suddenly, a panicked look on her face. 'Will I still see Bo Bo?'

'Of course,' I smiled. 'You and Bo can still see each other. We can go to Angela's house or perhaps she could come here. We'll make sure of that.'

Liz had already been round to Angela's house to tell Bo the same thing. Apparently she had taken the news really well and hadn't seemed particularly fazed. I often found the younger children were, the more adaptable they were.

'If I'm not going back to Mummy's, then where am I going to live?' asked Billie.

Liz and I exchanged glances.

'Nothing's going to change at the moment, Billie,' Liz told her. 'For now, you're going to stay here at Maggie's. Is that OK?'

Billie nodded.

'But where's Mummy and Uncle Jim going?' she asked, looking confused.

'I don't know,' replied Liz, honestly. 'They're adults so they can live where they want because they take care of themselves.'

I could see Billie was processing everything in her mind. That night when I was tucking her into bed, she had more questions.

'Can Bo come back and live here with us again, Maggie?' she asked me.

I shook my head.

'Not at the moment, flower,' I told her. 'The judge thought it was best that Bo stays with Angela.

'Maybe not for always, but for now. We still all need to do lots of talking.'

'We're always doing talking,' sighed Billie, looking weary.

As I stroked her long dark hair and said goodnight, I was suddenly struck by an overwhelming sense of guilt again. How on earth were we going to tell Billie that she wasn't going to stay with me long-term? How would she react to the news that I was moving her on?

She'd been through so much, and I wondered if I could really do that to her. I went downstairs and had another little cry, but I tried to remember Becky's words – *you have a right to have a life of your own, Maggie.*

I knew she was right, but when the time came to say goodbye, I knew my heart would break.

SEVENTEEN

The Perfect Pair

Sometimes in fostering everything happens at once; other times, weeks can go by with no new developments. It felt like so much had happened recently and I was glad of a few quiet weeks of respite.

Billie went to school, we saw Bo at Angela's a couple of times a week and started the reduced contact with Mandy. At least everyone knew what was happening now. Both girls had been told they weren't going back to live with their mum and Mandy had been told that that's what Social Services were going to recommend to the court. I always felt for birth parents being told this devastating news. No matter what had happened in the past, I couldn't even begin to imagine how it must feel to be told that you were losing custody of your children.

I didn't envy Liz having to break news like that.

'How did Mandy handle it?' I asked her when she called.

'She was full of childish excitement about going to court because she's never been before,' she sighed. 'I'm not sure that she fully understood why she was going to court and that effectively she was losing custody of her children.'

I felt sad for Mandy. If the court felt that she didn't fully understand the implications of the court case then they could appoint an appropriate adult. It was someone who supported vulnerable adults to make sure they understood their rights and to guide them through the legal process.

A few days later, the contact sessions with Mandy and the girls resumed at the contact centre. Billie and Bo had carried on seeing each other over the past few weeks and they were always pleased to see each other. In a way, living apart had taken the pressure off their relationship. Bo seemed a lot more relaxed around her big sister and her fear had gone.

'Hi, Bo Bo,' smiled Billie as she came running into the contact room.

Bo looked delighted to see her sister too and they sat down together on the floor and started playing with Barbies.

'I like it better when I come to your house,' Billie told her. 'Cos then I get to see Ziggy.'

'I love Ziggy,' smiled Bo.

'Well, we came here today because you're seeing Mummy,' I smiled. 'You haven't seen her for a while.'

As had often happened in the past, Mandy was late. Despite everything that Billie now knew, both girls still seemed pleased to see their mum and they ran over to her when she arrived.

'I'm sorry, girls, I ain't bought nothing for you to eat today,' she sighed. 'Liz the meanie wouldn't let me.'

Bo hugged her legs.

'We haven't seen you for a long, long time,' Billie told her.

'Don't be silly,' Mandy told her. 'It hasn't been that long. I bet you've been having a lovely time at your other houses.'

The more I saw of Mandy, the more I felt sorry for her. It was becoming increasingly obvious that she was a victim too in all of this, especially if it turned out that her own brother was the girl's father.

In terms of that, everything had gone quiet on the police front too, until Liz called me one morning.

'I've just had an update from Jemma,' she told me.

I listened intently as she described how the police had been planning to obtain a court order to get a DNA test from Jim.

'Before they could do that, though, he admitted it, Maggie,' she told me. 'He's the biological father of both girls.'

'Oh no,' I sighed, my stomach sinking.

At the back of my mind, it was what we'd all been expecting, but somehow I'd hoped that it wasn't true.

'What on earth are we going to say to the girls?' I asked her. 'How are we going to tell Billie?'

Liz said she had spoken at length to her manager about it and they'd also consulted a child psychologist.

'We've made the decision not to tell the girls right now,' she said. 'In time we will, but we've decided that they don't need to know at this moment in time when they're already coping with so much upheaval and change.'

'I think it's the right decision,' I replied.

There was nothing to be gained by telling them now. They were both too young to understand the complexities of adult relationships and what it meant, particularly Bo, who was still so young. It could be done over time with the help of a therapist when Social Services felt they were old enough to understand.

What Jim's admission did mean, though, was that the police were going to pursue an incest prosecution against Mandy and Jim.

They were still considering whether they were going to charge Mandy with sexual assault of a child.

It was only when I put the phone down that the realisation hit me that Billie probably wouldn't be living with me when she was told that her Uncle Jim was her biological father. I felt an overwhelming sense of sadness that it would be something that another carer was going to guide her through.

I just hoped that whoever Social Services found to foster Billie, they would be committed to her. As she got older, she was going to need a lot of help to understand what had happened to her. If a child has a committed carer then often that's half the battle won.

While all this was going on, Liz was still looking for a new carer to take Billie on long-term. We were all realistic about the fact it wasn't going to happen overnight, and I was happy to keep Billie on for as long as that took. I knew that, like me, anyone she found would have to be happy to only foster Billie.

She kept me regularly updated.

'I'm trying, Maggie,' she told me. 'I really am. I'm looking in other boroughs and all around the country.'

I knew none of us wanted to move Billie to a family too far away, as it was important for her to still see Bo regularly.

'There's no rush,' I replied. 'Billie's OK where she is for now.'

Louisa's bump was getting bigger by the day but I couldn't rush anything for Billie's sake. I wouldn't be happy unless I knew she had gone to the right people.

It will *happen*, I told myself.

And three weeks later, to my relief, it did.

'Maggie,' gasped Liz as she rung me one afternoon. 'I think I've just found the perfect carers for Billie.'

I listened with bated breath as she told me about them. Gillian and David were in their early sixties and lived around forty-five minutes from me. They had two grown-up sons and they'd been fostering for the past ten years.

'They're happy to foster one child,' she told me. 'But the amazing thing is, they've had specialist training to foster children who have been sexually abused or are abusers themselves.'

She described how previously they'd fostered a teenage boy who'd been taken into care after sexually abusing his younger sister.

'Talking to them, they said that it had been a huge challenge and a steep learning curve, but he was with them for five years until he went into assisted living,' she told me. 'When I told them about Billie, they seemed very open to meeting you and hearing more about her. Unlike a lot of other carers that I've spoken to, they're not fazed by the sexual abuse at all and they're well-equipped to help support Billie and continue all the work that you've been doing with her, Maggie.'

From what Liz was saying, they seemed ideal, and we arranged to go round and see them the following week.

Liz came to pick me up one morning after I'd dropped Billie at school. I was intrigued to meet them but I felt incredibly nervous too. I wanted them to be right and I also wanted them to want Billie. As a foster carer, you invest so much in every child that comes through your door and you just want the best for them.

'Did they ask why I wasn't keeping Billie long-term?' I asked Liz.

'I explained the situation to them and they completely understood. One child is ideal for them but they know that it's not for everyone.

'Maggie, no one is judging you,' she promised.

'I don't think I'll ever stop feeling guilty,' I sighed.

I'd never been to the village where Gillian and David lived but it was a pretty little place with lots of open countryside around it.

'Billie will have to change schools,' I said, and Liz nodded.

'That might not be such a bad thing,' she replied. 'There's a school in the village and it's much smaller, so perhaps it would be easier for them to manage the safeguarding measures.'

I was expecting Gillian and David to live in a cottage but their house was a new build on an estate at the edge of the village. As we rang the doorbell, I heard a dog barking.

'They've got a dog,' I smiled to Liz. 'Billie would love that.'

When the door opened, two little Yorkshire terriers ran towards us, wagging their tails enthusiastically.

'Two dogs, in fact!' I laughed.

A woman stood in the doorway. She was a tiny little bird-like woman with short, cropped white hair.

Liz had spoken to Gillian and David on the phone and had got lots of information about them but she hadn't met them in person yet.

'I'm Liz,' she told the woman. 'Nice to meet you, Gillian.'

'You too,' she smiled. 'And you must be Maggie. Come on in.'

'David's in the kitchen,' she told us. 'And you've already met Pixie and Trixie.'

'Billie has been desperate for a dog for ages so she would love these two,' I told her.

'We've got a cat called Barry as well but he's not a big fan of these two, so he makes himself scarce most of the time,' she smiled.

I could already tell she had a lovely, warm nature and I had a good feeling about her.

David was in the kitchen making a pot of coffee. He was like a male version of Gillian – short and slim with matching white hair. He gave my hand a firm shake.

'Nice to meet you, Maggie,' he told me. 'And hello, Liz.'

We all went through to the conservatory at the back of the house that overlooked open fields.

'What a lovely view,' I sighed.

'Yes, we're very lucky,' said David. 'I sit here for ages with my paper watching all the birds. We sometimes get deer too.'

We all sipped our coffees, chatting politely.

'So what can you tell us about Billie, Maggie?' Gillian asked. 'Liz has told us a bit but it's always good to talk to the child's current carer as they know them the best.'

I thought it was important to give them an honest picture of Billie. I told them how she had arrived at my house. I explained about her not being toilet trained and the struggles we'd had with the girls' weight and the rickets.

'Gosh, I didn't think people still got rickets,' sighed Gillian, shaking her head.

'Me neither,' I said. 'She doesn't have it any more though and hopefully there aren't any long-term issues with her bones.'

I told them about the progress we'd made with eating and Billie's weight.

'She's still bigger than most children her age, but she's not obese,' I told them.

'Maggie has worked wonders,' Liz told them, smiling.

'It sounds like it,' smiled David.

I got out my phone and showed them some pictures of Billie.

'Ah, what a sweetheart,' smiled Gillian. 'She looks lovely. Look, David,' she told him, passing him the phone.

Then we moved onto the tricky part – the sexual abuse.

'I've explained to Gillian and David about Billie's family background,' Liz said. 'They understand that Billie was abused by her own mother and has gone on to abuse her sister.'

'Poor little lass,' tutted Gillian, shaking her head.

'I'm sure you know yourselves from the training you've had that it's learned behaviour,' I told them.

'If some of the only times a child experiences warmth and nurture is when they're being sexually abused then they will actively seek it out. It becomes almost a comfort thing. I think that's why Billie did it to Bo.'

David nodded and I could see tears in Gillian's eyes as I spoke.

I told them how Billie had never shown abusive behaviour towards any other child.

'Until we uncovered the abuse, Billie didn't even know that what she was doing was wrong,' I continued. 'Luckily she does understand that now and we've been doing lots of work around bodies and safe and unsafe touching and I think she really gets it.

'I'm confident that, in time, her behaviour can be changed.'

'She's only seven,' nodded Gillian. 'She's already been through so much.'

'Liz told us about the incest too,' added David.

I nodded.

'She's going to need a lot of help and therapy as she gets older to cope with everything,' I replied.

While David made some more coffee for everyone, Gillian told me a little bit more about themselves. They loved walking and playing tennis and had lots of friends in the village. To be honest, they didn't need to sell themselves to me. After half an hour in their company, I was already sold. It was up to them now whether they wanted to take Billie on or not.

'See you soon, hopefully,' I told them as we left.

'What do you think?' Liz asked as we drove away.

'I think they're wonderful,' I smiled. 'They just seem like really nice, kind people. I think Billie would love it there.'

'Do you think their age is an issue?' asked Liz.

'I don't see why it should be,' I told her. 'They both seem to be very fit, active people.

'I think it would be good for Billie. They'd encourage her to walk the dogs and go on bike rides.'

Liz and I were convinced they were right for Billie but now it was up to them to decide.

'I don't think I'll be able to sleep tonight,' I sighed. 'I just want them to say yes.'

'All we can do is wait,' said Liz.

It was four long days before Liz got back to me. It was a simple text written in capital letters.

THEY SAID YES!!!!

I was so relieved and delighted. But after that initial joy came a sense of sadness too.

Billie was really leaving, it was really happening.

With a child Billie's age, handovers to other carers were done quickly, often in a matter of days in fact. It wasn't like an adoption where there was lots of paperwork and court orders to process, and as Gillian and David were already existing carers, they'd had all their checks, which made it even speedier.

The first thing that needed to happen was to tell Billie. Liz came over after school the next day. It was what I'd been dreading all along and I swallowed the lump in my throat as Liz began to speak. We were all sitting in the living room and I'd turned the TV off.

'So, I'm here today because we need to talk to you about where you're going to live, Billie,' Liz told her gently.

'I live here, silly,' laughed Billie, and I felt another wave of guilt flood through me.

'Well, Maggie's going to be really, really busy soon because Louisa's going to have a baby and she needs Maggie's help.

'Maggie might even stay at Louisa's for a few weeks after the baby's born to help her out.'

Billie looked at me curiously and I nodded, trying to keep my expression neutral.

'So we thought it would be a good idea for us to find you another carer who wasn't as busy,' Liz continued.

'And we've found a lovely lady called Gillian who's married to a man called David and they live in a house in the countryside.

'They've got a bedroom all ready for a little girl who's around seven.'

Billie looked at me excitedly.

'I'm seven, Maggie!' she yelled.

'Yes, that's what I told them,' nodded Liz. 'And they wondered whether you'd like to come and visit their house and say hello.'

Billie paused, her face crumpled in concentration.

'Have they got a doggy?' she asked.

'Yes,' Liz smiled. 'They've actually got two dogs.'

'Two?' gasped Billie in amazement.

'Yep,' nodded Liz. 'They're called Pixie and Trixie and they really, really want someone to come and live with them who can help them look after the dogs and take them for walks.'

'Yes!' said Billie, jumping up and down. 'I can walk them. I'd be really good at that. I've held the lead for Ziggy at Bo Bo's house, haven't I?

'They've got two doggies, Maggie,' she told me excitedly.

'I know,' I smiled. 'And they've got a cat called Barry too.'

Billie giggled at his name.

'Would you like to go and meet them tomorrow after school?' asked Liz and Billie nodded her head eagerly.

Liz and I had a quick chat before she left.

'Well, that went better than I expected,' she told me.

'I think she's excited,' I replied. 'I hope she feels the same way tomorrow.'

That first meeting between a child and prospective foster parents was always a little nerve-wracking as you could never be sure about how it was going to go or how a little one was going to respond.

But to my relief, Billie still seemed excited when I picked her up after school the following day.

'Are we going to see Pixie and Trixie now?' she asked.

'Yes, and don't forget we'll be seeing Gillian and David too,' I told her.

Billie kept bombarding me with questions for the duration of the drive, and was practically bouncing up and down in her seat in excitement. But when we got there and knocked at the door, Billie suddenly became very shy, holding tight to my leg.

When Gillian opened it, she pressed herself into me and I put my arm around her for reassurance.

'Hello,' smiled Gillian. 'You must be Billie. We've heard lots about you. Do you want to come in and meet David?'

'Where are the doggies?' she asked her.

'They're in the kitchen,' Gillian told her. 'Would you like to come and meet them too?'

Billie nodded and followed me through the house, still firmly glued to my side.

As soon as the kitchen door opened and Billie saw the dogs, she ran over to them.

The three of us chatted while Billie played with the dogs.

'Would you like to see your bedroom?' asked Gillian and Billie nodded eagerly.

The dogs followed them upstairs, which Billie was delighted about. I stayed downstairs with David and he made us both a cup of tea. I could hear Billie shrieking and giggling upstairs.

'I think she likes her room,' I smiled.

'I think Gill has enjoyed getting it all nice for her,' he smiled. 'She went on a bit of a shopping spree. It's been a while since we've fostered a little girl,'

When they came back downstairs, Billie was beaming.

'The doggies were jumping on my bed, Maggie,' she told me excitedly.

'Can they sleep in my bedroom?' she asked Gillian.

'I'm afraid they sleep in their crates in the kitchen at night,' she told her. 'But they'll love to play with you during the day and curl up on your lap to watch television.'

'We like Barry the cat to come in at night otherwise they'd be all running around chasing each other,' David told her.

I could see Billie was fascinated by all this.

'I made a chocolate cake,' said Gillian. 'Would you like a slice, and maybe a cup of squash?'

Billie looked at me for permission and I nodded.

'Oh, lovely,' I grinned. 'I bet Billie would love a slice of cake. I know I would.'

'We've got something else we thought you might like,' David told her.

He went to a cupboard and carried out a large plastic box. Inside were three Barbies and loads of clothes and accessories.

'Liz told us that you like Barbies, so we thought you might like to play with these,' David added.

Billie looked ecstatic as she rummaged excitedly in the box, gasping at the different outfits.

'We struck lucky at the local charity shop,' Gillian whispered to me.

'She'll really love those,' I smiled.

Gillian got on the floor and started playing Barbies with Billie whilst David and I made small talk. Then David took her out into the garden and they threw a ball for the dogs. It was such a joy to see Billie running around in the garden and giggling at the two little dogs.

Gillian and I watched them through the window as they played.

'I think she's going to fit in here quite nicely,' she smiled.

'So do I,' I told her, meaning it.

When Billie came back in, she was really excited.

'Maggie, David says the doggies really like me because they brought the ball back to me,' she told me.

'That's amazing,' I smiled.

After an hour, we said our goodbyes. Past experience had taught me that an hour was about the right length of time for a first visit.

'Would you like to come back to our house for tea tomorrow?' Gillian asked her as we were leaving. 'We're hoping that you're going to be moving in with us quite soon but we thought it would be nice if you came to have tea with us first.'

Billie looked at me.

'Will you be coming, Maggie?' she asked me.

'Well, how about I come and pick you up from school and drop you off, but Gillian and David bring you back to our house?' I suggested.

'And what I can do is start pulling together some of your stuff so they can take some of it back with them for when you next come over.'

It was all moving quite quickly, but to my relief, Billie seemed absolutely fine with it all.

'What did you think?' I asked her on the way home. 'Did you like it at Gillian and David's house?'

She nodded.

'I liked the doggies lots and I like Gillian and David's white hair,' she told me.

As far as initial meetings go, it couldn't have gone any better. I just hoped it stayed that way over the next five days.

EIGHTEEN

Facing the Truth

I stuck the piece of paper on the pinboard above Billie's desk.

'There you go, lovey,' I told her. 'Now you know exactly when you're going to see Gillian and David.'

It was the morning after our first visit and I'd drawn her a wall chart to show her what was happening on each day.

'So, you're having tea with Gillian and David tonight,' I explained. 'Then tomorrow is Friday and it's your last day at school.'

'Will I see Gillian and David again?' she asked.

'Not tomorrow,' I told her. 'They thought you'd be tired after saying goodbye to all of your friends in your class.'

On Saturday, they were going to take Billie out for the morning and on the Sunday she was moving to their house.

I did worry when everything happened so quickly that children might get carried along by momentum and excitement. I knew that Billie was excited because everything was so new. I didn't think the reality had fully hit her yet that this was it and that she was really leaving. But whatever happened, I had such a good feeling about Gillian and David and I knew they'd support her through it.

At some point, Gillian and David would also meet Bo. We'd decided that once Billie was settled with them, after a few days they'd take her round to Angela's house and they would all introduce themselves.

The next couple of days went well although I could see poor Billie was exhausted. Even though she'd only been at school for a few months, Miss Senior and her classmates made her a lovely goodbye card and they'd written all their names on it.

'When is my last sleep here, Maggie? she asked me as we had dinner that night, her big blue eyes round.

'Tomorrow,' I told her. 'Then on Sunday morning Gillian and David are coming to collect you and take you back to your new house.'

'Will they bring Trixie and Pixie?' she asked.

'I don't think so, lovey,' I told her. 'But you'll see them when you get home.'

Home. It felt slightly strange saying it. But Gillian and David's house *was* going to be her new home.

'Does Mummy know that I'm going to Gillian and David's house?' she asked me.

Contact had already been reduced to once every two weeks, and although Mandy had been told Billie was moving placement, neither she nor the girls had mentioned it. In fact, Liz had said Mandy had seemed completely disinterested when she'd talked her through it and hadn't even asked why.

'Yes, Mummy knows that you're going to be living with Gillian and David, sweetie. And you'll still get to see her, even when you're living there.

'What shall we do on your last night?' I asked her. 'We could watch a movie together and have popcorn?'

She nodded eagerly.

I wanted to keep it very low key and make her final night with me a quiet and peaceful one. Sometimes I'd have a party or invite people round when a child left but it just didn't feel right in Billie's case. I felt having a party would raise her anxieties and hype her up. Also, to me, her leaving didn't feel like a celebration. Even though I knew I was doing it for the right reasons, I still felt responsible for a child having to move and it would take a long time for that guilt to go away.

The following morning, Gillian and David took Billie to a safari park and by the time she got back that evening, I'd packed up most of her stuff. I'd cooked her favourite tea of sausages and roast potatoes before we sat down to watch *Mary Poppins* together.

'I've got a little something for you,' I told her as I tucked her in that night.

I handed her a parcel and she ripped the wrapping paper off.

'It's a photo album,' I told her.

I'd filled it with lots of pictures of her time at my house.

'Look, it's me and Bo Bo,' she grinned as she flicked through it.

As we looked at the photographs together, I was shocked by how different both girls looked now. They'd lost so much weight in these past few months and the health visitor had proudly told me that they weren't considered obese any more.

We hadn't had any big adventures or days out or mingled with lots of people, but we'd done exactly what both girls needed – had lots of quiet time at home giving them the stability, the security and routine that they desperately craved. I knew there was still lots of healing for Billie to do, but whatever happened, she was hopefully leaving my house a happier, healthier child who was starting to understand that what had happened to her at the hands of her own mother was wrong.

'You can take the photo album with you to Gillian and David's,' I told her. 'Shall I pack it one of your boxes?'

Billie nodded.

She'd been very quiet tonight, and I knew she was starting to realise that tomorrow she was leaving for good.

'Night night, sleep tight,' I soothed. 'It's going to be an exciting day tomorrow, so make sure you get some sleep.

'I bet Pixie and Trixie are really looking forward to seeing you,' I added and she gave me a little smile.

Even though I was trying to keep a brave face on things for Billie, when I went downstairs I couldn't stop myself from having a little cry.

I knew it was best to get it out of my system now rather than in the morning in front of Billie. I made myself a hot chocolate and rang Vicky for a pep talk.

'I feel so selfish,' I sighed. 'I shouldn't be letting her go.'

'Maggie, you're allowed to have a life, and you know there are so many more children that are going to need you,' she told me kindly. 'And Billie will be absolutely fine. Her new carers sound lovely.'

I'd been over and over it in my mind so many times but I knew there were no other possible options. It was hard, but in my heart of hearts, I knew it was the best thing for everyone.

The next morning, Billie was still very quiet but I rallied her round.

'Come on,' I told her. 'Let's get you out of those pyjamas so we can pack them for you to take.'

I still had lots to do before Gillian and David arrived at 10 a.m., so the first couple of hours of the day were a flurry of activity, gathering up all of the last bits and pieces for Billie to take with her. I didn't mind, as it stopped me dwelling on what was about to happen.

When I heard the knock at the door just before ten, I was putting the final few things into a box. I took a deep breath and steeled myself.

You can do this, Maggie, I told myself firmly.

Saying goodbye was always so hard, but this one felt particularly raw, perhaps because I felt like I had caused it.

'Come on, Billie,' I told her. 'Gillian and David are here.'

She jumped up and ran to the door and gave them both a big hug.

'Are you ready then, sweetheart?' Gillian asked her, smiling.

'Nearly,' she said.

We all carried the last few boxes to the car. Before she got into the back seat, Billie flung her arms around me and gave me the tightest squeeze.

'I'm going to miss you,' I told her, blinking back tears. 'But I'll phone you in a couple of days to see how you're getting on.'

She nodded sadly, and waved at me as she walked towards the car.

'Can we take the doggies for a walk today?' she asked David a she climbed into the back seat.

'Yes,' he smiled. 'We can take them out when we get back, although we've got a bit of unpacking to do first by the looks of it.'

Gillian came over and put her arm around me.

'She's going to be just fine,' she told me and I nodded.

Even though I'd put on my best 'happy' face for Billie, Gillian could tell that inside I was having a wobble.

'Thank you,' I told her. 'I know you'll look after her.'

I took a deep breath as Gillian walked back down the path, and I did what I had to do. I stood on the pavement and forced the biggest smile I could muster as the car pulled away. David had opened the window on Billie's side so the last thing I saw was her chubby little hand waving to me.

I walked back into the house, which suddenly seemed deathly quiet. It had only been two of us but Billie and I had been a close little pair these last few months and I missed her already.

There's a part of you that gets so used to having these little people around all day that it's a real wrench when they leave. I knew that it was going to take a few days for it to sink in, and I had to accept the difficult feelings, knowing that Billie was really gone for good.

Louisa and Charlie, bless them, had invited me round for Sunday lunch as they knew I'd need cheering up. It was lovely to see them both, and as I listened to Louisa chatting excitedly about the baby, I knew in my heart that I had made the right decision. I was so excited about my new grandchild, and I knew that I owed it to Louisa, and to myself, to be able to fully immerse myself in helping look after this new baby.

On Monday morning, Becky phoned.

We had a chat about Billie and how the goodbye had gone, and how she'd been settling in at Gillian and David's.

'So, you've got an empty house again, Maggie! Shall I put you back on the emergency placement list now?' she asked me.

I thought about it for a minute.

'Not for now,' I told her. 'I think I'm going to take a little break.'

Louisa's baby was due in less than four weeks and I wanted to be there for her to help out when the time came.

'I think I'm going to concentrate on being a nana for a bit,' I told her. 'And just enjoy the sunshine while I wait.'

It was a lovely summer's day and I'd made plans to catch up with Graham later and meet my friend Carol for a coffee.

'I don't blame you, Maggie,' Becky told me. 'You deserve it. It's been an intense few months.'

It really had. Being a foster carer was at the heart of who I was, but I knew that in order to be able to support the next child or children that came into my life, it was important to give myself a chance to take a breath and reflect on all that had happened.

A couple of weeks later, I was hoovering the hallway when something came through the letterbox and thudded onto the doormat. It was the local paper. To be honest, it usually went straight into the recycling bin, but as I picked it up, the headline on the front page caught my eye.

Brother and sister admit incest.

My heart started thumping and, with shaking hands, I sat down on the stairs so that I could read it. Neither of the defendants had been named as there was a court order protecting their identities, but I knew from the moment I saw the headline that it was Mandy and Jim.

The article said they'd both pleaded guilty to two charges of sexual activity with a family member. Neither of them could refute the charges because DNA tests had proved that they were the parents of two children.

The court had heard that the two siblings had been brought up in a dysfunctional home where they had also been subjected to incest and sexual abuse. The article stated that Mandy and Jim's mother had been in a sexual relationship with her own father and Mandy had been abused by her own mother. The court heard that she had learning difficulties and was particularly vulnerable.

What Mandy and Jim had done was horrendous, but it was clear from reading this sad tale that neither of them had ever stood a chance. No one had ever told them what was right and wrong so they knew no other way. The court had heard both their grandfather and their mother had died several years ago so all they'd had left was each other. They'd each received a twelve-month suspended sentence.

What they'd done was wrong, but I was glad, reading about their own backgrounds, that neither of them had gone to prison. I didn't think that would help either of them. Ultimately, their children had been taken away from them and that was the greatest punishment of all.

Their story felt like a jigsaw that we'd been slowly putting together over the past few months. Now we'd finally got the last few pieces and it was all desperately sad. Knowing what had happened to Mandy in the past made me see that she hadn't stood a chance. She'd parented the only way she knew how, based on her own childhood. We can't ever change the past, but I was confident Billie and Bo could change their futures. With a lot of help, they could finally break the cycle of abuse and make new lives for themselves, away from the dysfunction of their birth family.

I spoke to Billie every few days and things were going well. She still had lots of hurdles to cope with, though. She would only realise the enormity of what had happened to her as she got older. She and Bo would also have to cope with learning that Jim was their biological father when the time was right. It would take a lot of effort, therapy and support, but they could do it.

Reading about the court case in the paper had been a real shock, so that afternoon I decided to do some knitting to help take my mind off things. I couldn't help myself, and Louisa's baby already had quite the outfit collection.

I was just starting a little pink woollen hat when my mobile rang.

It was Louisa.

'I was just thinking about you,' I told her.

'Oh, Maggie,' she gasped.

The desperate tone of her voice filled me with instant dread.

'What is it, lovey?' I asked. 'What's happened? Are you OK?'

'I think the baby's coming, Maggie,' she panted. 'It really hurts. I've had niggling pains all day but I thought I'd just over-done it doing some decorating. But they're getting worse.'

Panic pulsed through me.

'OK, stay right where you are, flower, and I'll come round right now,' I told her urgently. 'Have you rung Charlie?'

'It went to voicemail so I left a message,' she said, bursting into tears. 'He's at work.'

'It's too early, Maggie,' she sobbed. 'She's not due for another four weeks. What if something happens to her?'

'Hold on, flower,' I told her. 'Just hold on. We'll get you to hospital and it's going to be fine.'

'Please hurry,' she wailed.

'Keep doing your breathing and I'll be there in ten minutes,' I assured her.

I grabbed my keys and my handbag and ran out the door in blind panic.

Louisa and Charlie's flat was only a ten-minute drive from my house but it felt like for ever.

'Come on,' I urged as I crept along behind a learner driver. *Please let her be OK. Please let her be OK.*

The moment I pressed the doorbell, Louisa buzzed me in and I bolted up the stairs. She was waiting inside the open front door, holding onto the hallway wall for support.

'Oh, lovey,' I gasped. 'How are you doing?'

'I'm OK,' she sighed. 'The contractions have eased off a little bit but when they come they're still bad.'

I put my arm around her for support and led her into the living room. She was in pain but she seemed a lot calmer now that she wasn't on her own. I got her to squeeze my hand when the next one came and talked her through it. When it was over, she slumped back on the sofa in relief.

Suddenly her phone rang and she asked me to answer it. Thankfully it was Charlie.

'You need to come home,' I told him. 'Louisa's in labour.'

I could hear the panic in his voice.

'She's OK,' I added. 'Just get back here as quick as you can and I'll drive you both to the hospital.'

I could see the relief on Louisa's face.

'As soon as Charlie gets here, we'll get your bag and I'll take you to hospital, OK?'

Louisa nodded but I could see tears welling up in her eyes.

'It's just so early, Maggie,' she sighed. 'She's going to be so little.'

I grabbed her hand and gave it a reassuring squeeze.

'It's going to be fine,' I soothed. 'I'll get you to the hospital and the midwives and doctors are going to look after you and do everything they can to make sure you and the baby are healthy.

'Your scans have shown she's already a good weight and soon you're going to be able to meet her.'

'I know,' smiled Louisa. 'I can't wait.'

'She's going to be absolutely fine, and so are you. Just you wait and see.'

I squeezed her hand, filled with excitement for the happy times that lay ahead for her and Charlie and our growing family.

Acknowledgements

Thank you to my children, Tess, Pete and Sam, who are such a big part of my fostering today – however, I had not met you when Billie and Bo came into my home. To my wide circle of fostering friends – you know who you are! Your support and your laughter are valued. To my friend Andrew B for your continued encouragement and care. Thanks also to Heather Bishop, who spent many hours listening and enabled this story to be told, my literary agent Rowan Lawton and to Anna Valentine and Marleigh Price at Seven Dials for giving me the opportunity to share these stories.

A Note from Maggie

I really hope you enjoyed reading these stories. I love sharing my experiences of fostering with you, and I also love hearing what you think about them. If you enjoyed this book, or any of my others, please think about leaving a review online. I know other readers really benefit from your thoughts, and I do too.

To be the first to hear about my new books, you can keep in touch on my Facebook page @MaggieHartleyAuthor. I find it inspiring to learn about your own experiences of fostering and adoption, and to read your comments and reviews.

Finally, thank you so much for choosing to read *Is It My Fault Mummy?* If you enjoyed it, there are others available including *Too Scared to Cry, Tiny Prisoners, The Little Ghost Girl, A Family for Christmas, Too Young to be a Mum, Who Will Love Me Now, The Girl No One Wanted, Battered, Broken, Healed, Sold to be a Wife, Denied a Mummy, Daddy's Little Soldier* and *Please Don't Take My Sisters.* I hope you'll enjoy my next story just as much.

Maggie Hartley

Credits

Maggie Hartley and Seven Dials would like to thank everyone at Orion who worked on the publication of *A Sister's Shame*.

Editorial
Marleigh Price

Copy editor
Clare Wallis

Proofreader
Sarah Hulbert

Audio
Paul Stark
Amber Bates

Contracts
Anne Goddard
Paul Bulos
Jake Alderson

Design
Rachael Lancaster
Joanna Ridley
Nick May

Editorial Management
Jane Hughes

Finance
Jasdip Nandra
Afeera Ahmed
Elizabeth Beaumont
Sue Baker

Marketing
Lucy Cameron

Production
Claire Keep

Publicity
Kate Moreton

Sales
Laura Fletcher
Esther Waters
Victoria Laws
Rachael Hum

DADDY'S LITTLE SOLDIER

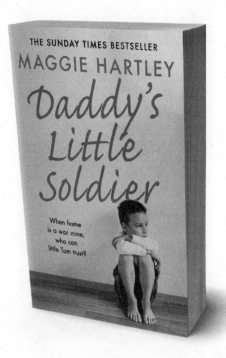

Tom has been taken into care following concerns that his dad is struggling to cope after the death of Tom's mum. When Maggie meets Tom's dad Mark, a stern ex-soldier and strict disciplinarian, it's clear that Tom's life at home without his mummy has been a constant battlefield. Can Maggie help Mark to raise a son and not a soldier? Or is little Tom going to lose his daddy too?

PLEASE, DON'T TAKE MY SISTERS

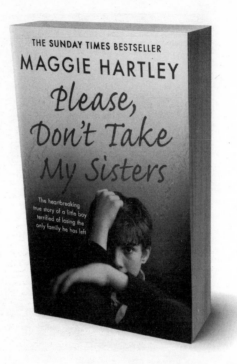

Leo's little sisters are the only family he has left in the world. But when Social Services begin to look at rehoming the little girls without their troubled older brother, the siblings' whole world comes crashing down. Can Maggie fight to keep the children together? Or will Leo lose the only love he's ever known?

A DESPERATE CRY FOR HELP

Meg arrives at Maggie's after a fire destroys the children's home she's been living in. But traumatised by the fire, and angry and vulnerable, having been put into care by her mother, Meg is lashing out at everyone around her. Can Maggie reach this damaged little girl before it's too late? And before Meg's destructive behaviour puts Maggie's life – and the lives of the other children in her care – at risk?

TINY PRISONERS

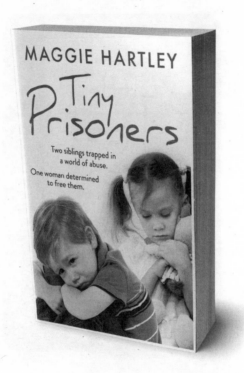

Evie and Elliot are scrawny, filthy and wide-eyed with fear when they turn up on foster carer Maggie Hartley's doorstep. They're too afraid to leave the house and any intrusion of the outside world sends them into a panic. It's up to Maggie to unlock the truth of their heart-breaking upbringing, and to help them learn to smile again.

THE LITTLE GHOST GIRL

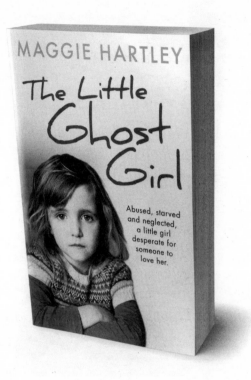

Ruth is a ghost of a girl when she arrives into foster mother Maggie Hartley's care. Pale, frail and withdrawn, it's clear to Maggie that Ruth had seen and experienced things that no 11-year-old should have to. Ruth is in desperate need of help, but can Maggie get through to her and unearth the harrowing secret she carries?

TOO YOUNG TO BE A MUM

When sixteen-year-old Jess arrives on foster carer Maggie Hartley's doorstep with her newborn son Jimmy, she has nowhere else to go. With social services threatening to take baby Jimmy into care, Jess knows that Maggie is her only chance of keeping her son. Can Maggie help Jess learn to become a mum?

WHO WILL LOVE ME NOW?

At just ten years old, Kirsty has already suffered a lifetime of heartache and suffering. When her latest foster carers decide they can no longer cope, Kirsty comes to live with Maggie. Reeling from this latest rejection, the young girl is violent and hostile, and Social Services fear that she may be a danger to those around her. Maggie finds herself in an impossible position, one that calls into question her decision to become a foster carer in the first place...

BATTERED, BROKEN, HEALED

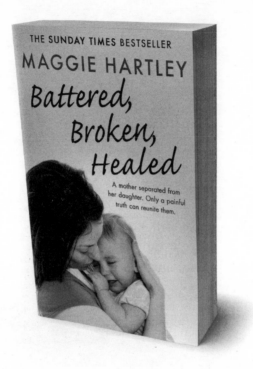

Six-week-old baby Jasmine comes to stay with Maggie after she is removed from her home. Neighbours have repeatedly called the police on suspicion of domestic violence, but her timid mother Hailey vehemently denies that anything is wrong. Can Maggie persuade Hailey to admit what's going on behind closed doors so that mother and baby can be reunited?

SOLD TO BE A WIFE

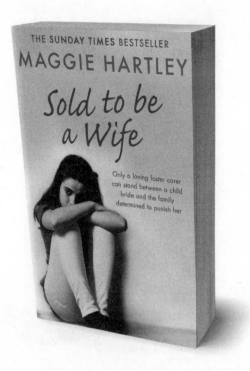

Fourteen-year-old Shazia has been taken into care over a fears that her family are planning to send her to Pakistan for an arranged marriage. But with Shazia denying everything and with social services unable to find any evidence, Shazia is eventually allowed to return home. But when Maggie wakes up a few weeks later in the middle of the night to a call from the terrified Shazia, it looks like her worst fears have been confirmed...

DENIED A MUMMY

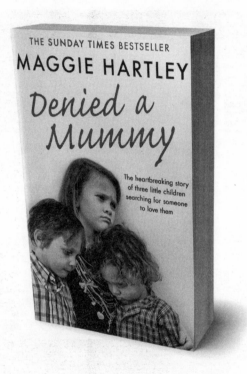

Maggie has her work cut out for her when her latest placement arrives on her doorstep; two little boys, aged five and seven and their eight- year-old sister. Having suffered extensive abuse and neglect, Maggie must slowly work through their trauma with love and care. But when a couple is approved to adopt the siblings, alarm bells start to ring. Maggie tries to put her own fears to one side but she can't shake the feeling of dread as she waves goodbye to them. Will these vulnerable children ever find a forever family?

TOO SCARED TO CRY

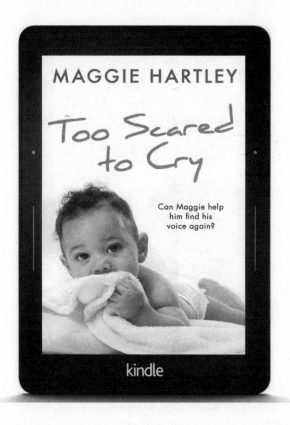

A baby too scared to cry. Two toddlers too scared to speak. This is the dramatic short story of three traumatised siblings, whose lives are transformed by the love of foster carer Maggie Hartley.

A FAMILY FOR CHRISTMAS

A tragic accident leaves the life of toddler Edward changed forever and his family wracked with guilt. Will Maggie be able to help this family grieve for the son they've lost and learn to love the little boy he is now? And will Edward have a family to go home to at Christmas?

THE GIRL NO ONE WANTED

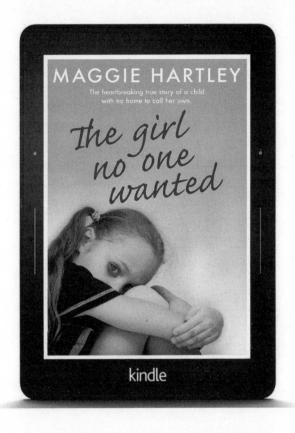

Eleven-year-old Leanne is out of control. With over forty placements in her short life, no local foster carers are willing to take in this angry and damaged little girl. Maggie is Leanne's only hope, and her last chance. If this placement fails, Leanne will have to be put in a secure unit. Where most others would simply walk away, Maggie refuses to give up on the little girl who's never known love.

IS IT MY FAULT MUMMY?

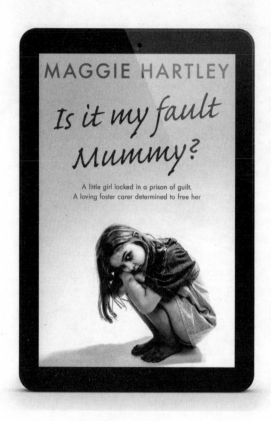

Seven-year-old Paris is trapped in a prison of guilt. Devastated after the death of her baby brother, Joel, Maggie faces one of the most heartbreaking cases yet as she tries to break down the wall of guilt surrounding this damaged little girl.